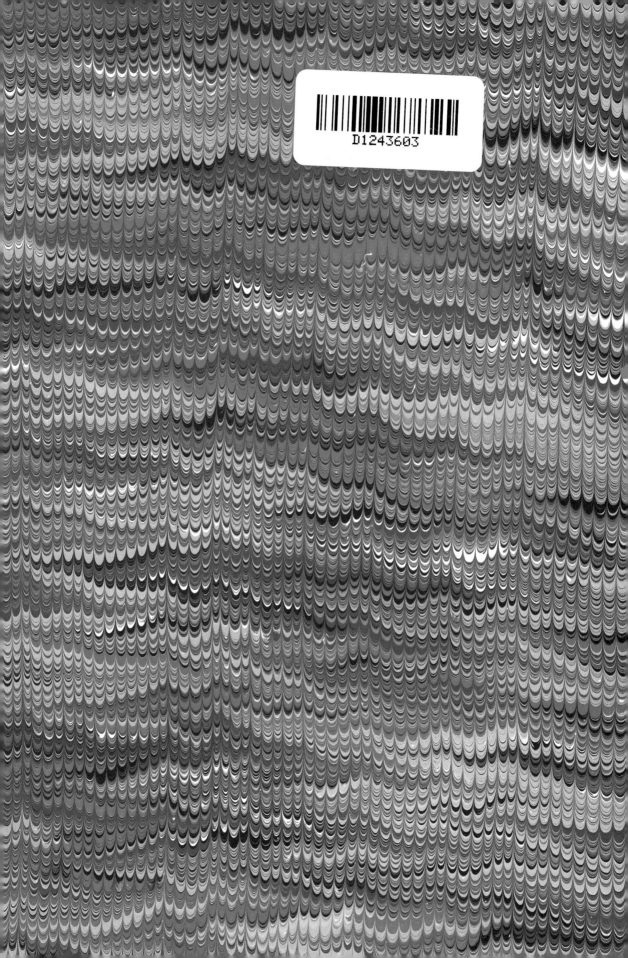
D1243603

Stefan Steigerwald / Ernst G. Siebeneicher-Hellwig

FANCY KNIVES

Materials and Decorative Techniques

FANCY KNIVES

Materials and
Decorative Techniques

Stefan Steigerwald / Ernst G. Siebeneicher-Hellwig

4880 Lower Valley Road, Atglen, Pennsylvania 19310

Front Cover: Fully integral knife by W. Schirmer with Bruyere wood inlays / Folding knife by S. Steigerwald with Damascene blade and meteoric iron-titanium handle / Reindeer-horn knife by W. Biegi with traditional structure and design / Fully integral knife by S. Steigerwald of Damascene steel with mother-of-pearl inlays.

The authors, the publishers and their representatives cannot be held responsible for personal, material or factual damage.

Schiffer Books are available at special discounts for bulk purchases for sales promotions or premiums. Special editions, including personalized covers, corporate imprints, and excerpts can be created in large quantities for special needs. For more information contact the publisher:

Published by Schiffer Publishing Ltd.
4880 Lower Valley Road
Atglen, PA 19310
Phone: (610) 593-1777; Fax: (610) 593-2002
E-mail: Info@schifferbooks.com

For the largest selection of fine reference books on this and related subjects, please visit our web site at **www.schifferbooks.com**
We are always looking for people to write books on new and related subjects.
If you have an idea for a book please contact us at the above address.

This book may be purchased from the publisher.
Include $5.00 for shipping.
Please try your bookstore first.
wwYou may write for a free catalog.

In Europe, Schiffer books are distributed by
Bushwood Books
6 Marksbury Ave.
Kew Gardens
Surrey TW9 4JF England
Phone: 44 (0) 20 8392-8585; Fax: 44 (0) 20 8392-9876
E-mail: info@bushwoodbooks.co.uk
Website: www.bushwoodbooks.co.uk
Free postage in the U.K., Europe; air mail at cost.

Copyright © 2008 by Schiffer Publishing, Ltd.
Originally published as Messer Materiallien und Verschönerungstechniken by Motorbuch Verlag
Library of Congress Control Number: 2008927511

ISBN: 978-0-7643-3067-4
Printed in China

Contents

The Authors

The following specialists and authors collaborated on this book:

Alexandra Feodorow: knife engraver on a high (Ferlacher) level.

Eva Halat: born 1953, painter and Scrimshaw artist, author of the book *Modern Scrimshaw*.*

Horst Heinle: born 1937, specialist in ivory and mother-of-pearl, materials dealer.

Richard "Ritchi" Maier: born 1965, internationally renowned engraver, know for his especially fine engravings and Scrimshaw work.

Fred Schmalz: born 1949, industrial and locksmithing master, damascene steelsmith.

Ernst G. Siebeneicher-Hellwig: born 1950, hobby knifemaker and author of the book *Messermachen***.

Stefan Steigerwald: born 1968, professional knifemaker and materials dealer.

*   Published by Verlag Angelka Hoernig, Ludwigshafen, 2003.
** Published by Venatus Verlag, Braunschweig, 2000.
The photos were provided by the authors.

Acknowledgments

Along with the cited co-authors, special thanks go out to Mr. Manfred Ritzer, who photographed numerous knives and materials for this book, and Mr. Erwin Schneller for his help with the chapter on leather sheaths.

In addition, our thanks to all those who kindly lent us knives and materials, and to our families for their understanding for us and our knifemaking passion.

Nuremberg and Munich, November 2004

Stefan Steigerwald, Ernst G. Siebeneicher-Hellwig

The authors Stefan Steigerwald and Ernst G. Siebeneicher-Hellwig in their "natural" environment.

Foreword

Thoughts on Knives

Egon Trompeter,
ex-President of the German Knifemakers' Guild

People and knives have followed the same paths since ancient times. People needed a "cutting tool" to survive. It was their most important tool. It was also their most important weapon. With the sharp edges of the forged blade they carved the meat of the hunted animal, whose meat gave them nourishment and whose pelt warmed them. The "invention" of the knife thus became an important step in human history; it assured survival and provided for the successful further development of mankind.

One no longer needs a knife in order to stay alive today. Yet we cannot imagine our daily life without it. It has become an important component of our lives. Knives of the most varied kind accompany us. We are surrounded by eating, carving, and other kitchen knives. A mushroom collector's knife makes gathering food in the forest easier. We are accompanied by pocket knives and other useful kinds. Survival knives even assure our survival in the endless distances of dangerous wildlands.

But there are other reasons to buy knives. One possibility is a variation of the "desire to possess." There is collecting. One does not need it, one simply has it. Thus the subject of knives takes on a new and impressive aspect. An aspect that raises it from a simple utensil and weapon to an object of art. The knife as a fine collector's item.

The choice is great. Knives exist in the most varied forms and price ranges. Mass-produced or unique, handmade knives. The most varied handle and blade types. Steel and handle materials from the usual to the exotic. Special knives, utilitarian knives, knives to look at and to use. In fact, a lot has happened since the first flint blades.

Knife collectors and fans can often envision their ideal knife, but cannot find it in the marketplace. The difference between their conceptions and what is on the market is so great. One way around this situation is to have a knife made by a knifemaker. Dreams become reality. Desires are fulfilled. For there is a certain self-fulfillment in it. And in the end, that is what it's all about.

In this book by the well-known knifemakers, Stefan Steigerwald and Ernst Siebeneicher-Hellwig, the most varied aspects of the subject of knives are illuminated in detail. They lead the interested reader through the fascinating world of knives as cutting tools and weapons to objects of art.

Knife and Soul

Dr. Volker J. Geers,
Knife Collector

Reading this book is fun. There is information on the components of knives, their materials, and the various techniques. A *vademecum* for all knife fans. But is that all that is essential for their description and evaluation?

Collectors do not value their items for their material value, for knives have a soul above and beyond their substance.

What is the soul? The soul cannot be grasped, measured or described by scientific methods. Soul is a metaphor for life, the living part, in and of itself. Soul describes the self, the individual, the person or the vitality. Soul points to the internal, the intangible, the spirit, the feeling, the character.

All this can be made clear in reference to human beings. But can objects have a spirit or a soul?

A soul does not exist in empty space. It becomes clear only through acquaintance. Love sometimes comes at first sight. Someone recognizes the soul of the other and sees in it something beautiful, lovable, One looks into the eyes—or at the figure—and knows this is the right one.

Sometimes it does not go so fast and requires an initial spark. One is with someone for a long time, at work or in a club, and suddenly one recognizes after the other has said or done something: This is the one. This is what I have unknowingly been seeking for so long.

There is also a love at first sight among knives. One looks at it, holds it in one's hand, and it flows over one: The inner voice says, I like that. With knives too, there is this a developing love. One reads something about the maker, learns something about the used materials, the idea that the maker had of the function of the knife; and one recognizes—this one has class. I want this one.

Naturally this is different for every individual. One reacts quickly, another slowly, one to this, another to that. There is no formula.

The materials and techniques described in this book are possible ways to ignite that initial spark: The exotic material, the rare form of the blade, the function or the handle. But it may also be that the best technical or material combination is not enough to effect emotion. Such knives seem cold, simply soulless.

Whoever has held knives of the great ones in his hand knows what I mean. Bob Loveless gets better prices than his students, even though their knives are made objectively better. The knives of Michael Walker can be told from those of his imitators with closed eyes. The folders made by Ron Lake are always recognizable—not only by the sound—even when they lie beside others that look almost like them.

In Europe too, there are many knifemakers who give their works a soul. Unfortunately, though, there are also those who merely assemble them by rote and are surprised that their knives go nowhere. So knives have a soul. But how can the knifemaker breathe this soul into his products?

Introduction

Isn't it fascinating to work with materials and substances that make outsiders ask whether this belongs in a museum? Mammoth ivory, meteorites, fossils, semi-precious stones. The old smithing art is brought back to life by dedicated, capable artisans. Engravings so fine that, at first glance, one cannot grasp the artistic technique behind them.

How much time and love are present in something unique? Is it not precisely that which we need in these hectic times?

Many of the knives depicted in this book cost a lot of money. But how long were their makers busy bringing them into existence? Quite aside from their material value. The information in this book lets one sense it. Knives are not merely works of art, but also everyday utensils. They accompany us as do other everyday things of beauty: home furnishings, a nice watch, a noble pen. And the noble knife should also have this kind of value.

The "weapon" aspect plays a subordinate role here, which I would largely like to ignore.

A collector who knows materials knows more about his possessions. Misunderstanding is limited. And the knifemaker can save himself so much work through basic knowledge and practical experience.

Stefan Steigerwald

Making knives can become a passion, even an obsession. I came originally from painting. Painting a picture can be tremendously satisfying. But making knives fascinates through its variety. Just the variety of usable materials gives much room for creativity. In making the plan or design, one can inject his artistic blood. In the practice of making it real, the artisan and meticulous worker is required to use all of his abilities and skills.

Knifemakers learn constantly. They learn to know new materials and their properties, different means of working with them, and new tricks. Finally, they constantly add to their artistic capability.

When, after a long time, I held my first kit knife in my hand, I was horrified by the poor surface work with its many visible traces. I had been so proud of my work. But at that time I simply did not know any better.

For a finished knife, a first practical test quickly shows whether the cutting tool amounts to anything. The knifemaker can now add the finished piece to his collection, give it away or sell it. Most of the hobby knifemakers I know personally have already sold one knife or another. Many finance their hobby that way. Is it not truly ideal to be able to earn money from one's hobby? Most hobbies just cost money.

This book is meant to help the knife fan to practice his hobby more intensively. The collector will learn more about his knives and the materials of which they are made. The beginner will find valuable advice on how to making knives and what he needs to do so. For the hobby knifemaker, one or another tip may be helpful.

Finally, all knife fans can enjoy the beautiful pieces of work that are illustrated in the excellent color photographs in this book.

Ernst G. Siebeneicher-Hellwig

The "Oetzi Knife", a reproduction of the knife found in the ice with the glacier man.

Above: A dagger blade from the middle Bronze Age, Palestine.
Center: Reproduction of a knife from the late Bronze Age.
Below: A bronze horse from Etruria.

Materials

Steel

The oldest and hardest material of which man has made blades is stone (see upper left picture).

With the smelting of copper and tin, the basis was created for the alloying of bronze, the first useful metal (see lower left picture).

Although bronze knives provided very suitable cutting tools, only the working of hardened iron brought the breakthrough in the production of high-performance blades. Since the Iron Age—beginning in Anatolia around 1500 B.C.—iron has been the basis of our civilization. The Hittites, an Indo-European people, rank as the inventors of ironworking. The knowledge of ironworking reached central Europe only around 500 B.C. The German word *Eisen* and the English word *iron* both come from Celtic and presumably derived from the word *isara*: strong, firm. It was the Celts who first practiced the use and production of iron tools in Europe. The Celtic domination of pre-Christian northern and central Europe surely can be traced back to this. Whoever had iron weapons had the advantage in armed warfare.

A few words on iron in and of itself:
Iron, chemical symbol **Fe** from the Latin *ferrum*, is in its pure form a silvery-white, gleaming, easily bendable, relatively soft heavy metal. Its melting point is 1538° Celsius, its density 7.874 g/sq.cm. Pure iron is too soft for use. But the characteristics of iron can be influenced strongly by adding other metals, and particularly by adding carbon.

Modern tool steel has been available only since the invention of steel refining in the 19th century. We shall have a closer look at this material in what follows.

In order to understand what properties the various steels and groups of steels have, a short excursion into materials is necessary. For the user it is important to understand which properties he can expect from the steel he is using. Among the possible properties are lasting sharpness, flexibility, toughness, resistance to corrosion, hardness, and ability to be resharpened after use. The workability while making the knife, as well as the price of the steel, should not be ignored.

No steel can unite all the positive properties. A carbon steel that can be sharpened to a very keen edge, on account of its fine grain, is not very resistant to corrosion. A corrosion-resistant supersteel, made metallurgically from powder, may keep its sharpness to a high degree, but is difficult to sharpen and is expensive and laborious to work.

The steels suitable for making knives can be divided crudely into two groups:

The **carbon steels** and the **alloyed steels.**

Damascus steels will be treated in the section beginning on page 18, since they are partly mixed types and deserve special attention because of their technical specialties and high optical charm.

Carbon Steels

In principle, a steel chosen for making knives has to be able to be hardened. For that, a minimum amount, about 0.5%, of carbon in the steel is required. With a carbon content of over 1.7%, the iron can no longer be forged. Carbon steels lack other alloying elements (such as manganese, chromium, vanadium,, molybdenum, etc.) or have them only in unimportant traces.

Their properties include being "good-natured" in warm treatment and forging, that is, the steel forgives errors more easily and has a relatively large temperature range for forging and hardening. The workability in

an unhardened condition is good (filing, boring, grinding, etc.). The steel can be ground easily. Thanks to the fine grain of the iron carbide, the blade can be ground very finely.

The main weakness is the lack of resistance to rust. This property can be equalized somewhat by polishing to a high gloss and, naturally, by taking care of the material. In practice, this means cleaning the blade after use and oiling it lightly. But the best care cannot prevent the carbon steel from taking on a gray color in use and becoming flaky when it comes into contact with acids, such as fruit acids and apple peels or fatty acid from cutting pork roast.

One can recognize a carbon steel by the DIN norm number.

For example, **C50.** The C stands for carbon, the number 50 means 0.5% of carbon.

Usual Carbon Steels			
DIN	US Norm	Steel key	Properties
C45	1045	1.1193	Refined steel with 0.45% carbon
C55	1055	1.1209	Refined steel with 0.55% carbon
C60	1060	1.1221	Refined steel with 0.60% carbon
C100	1095	1.1274	Refined steel with 0.1% carbon

Alloyed Steels

The group of alloyed tool steels is ideal for making knives.

All members of this group have the positive qualities of rust-resistance (as long as they contain more than 13% chromium), high hardness in use, and staying sharp. The choice of the "right" steel depends mainly on the work that the knife is supposed to do.

For the so-called *Bavarian Lederhosen Knife,* the 440A is thoroughly suitable. It is easy to sharpen afterward, rust-resistant and not expensive. It does not hold its blade as well as, for example, its brother 440C, but when it is used as a bread knife, that is surely not the decisive criterion.

When high rust-resistance and good sharpening are wanted, 440C can be used. It is well suited to hunting knives or knives for maritime use, such as sailors' and shipboard knives. In tests, 440C has shown the highest values in terms of rust-resistance.

The AT534, a steel that is being used more and more often for high-priced knives, ranks somewhat behind 440C in rust-resistance, but it can clearly score in resistance to wear.

Powder-metallurgically produced steels (PM steels) score considerably better than ordinary steels in terms of resistance to wear. They can be highly hardened and yet retain good toughness. Three qualities that one certainly will want for knife steel. PM steels are used more and more in knifemaking, and for good reasons.

The PM steel is produced in a very complex process. The molten alloying materials are reduced to a fine powder under a vacuum or protective gas and then pressed together under high pressure and high temperature, making a doughy substance. Thanks to this process, alloying elements can be blended

that, in a molten state and in this high concentration, could not be mixed. This can be compared with salt and water: Salt can be dissolved easily in water, but if the limit of satiation is reached, no more salt dissolves. In addition, the hard carbide exists in the form of fine, uniform balls. Because of their very fine structure, PM steels can be polished very well.

Because of its great toughness or resistance to breaking, PM steel has greater safety reserves than conventional steel. One can utilize this gain by allowing greater hardness and making the cutting geometry thinner. The PM steel RWL34, which has the same composition as the traditional ATS34, can be hardened to a greater degree of Rockwell hardness without risk. The better mechanical properties allow a cutting angle up to three degrees flatter. This results in sharper blades with much greater resistance to dulling and breaking.

Powdered metal is also used in aeronautics for highly stressed turbine parts. Extreme temperatures and forces that prevail in the "hot" parts of a jet engine can be withstood only by materials made with powdered metal.

It becomes clear that PM steel, because of its complex production, is inherently more expensive than conventional cast steel. PM steels, because of their toughness and resistance to dulling, are hard to work and lead

Current Highly Alloyed Knife Steel Types

Designation	DIN Norm	C	CR	V	Mo
440A	X55CrMo4	0.6	19	-	1
440B	X90CrMoV18	0.9	19	-	1
440C	X105CrM017	1.2	18	-	1
ATS34	X100CrMo14 4	1	14	-	4
RWL-34	X110CrMoV14 5	1.1	14	3	5
ELMAX	X190CrMo17 3	19	17	3	1
D-2	X155CrVMo 12 1	1.5	12	1	0.8
O-1	X100MnCrW4	1	0.7	0.15	-
CPM-S30-V	X20CrV17 6	2.2	17	5.5	0.5, formerly CPM-440-V
CPM-S90-V	X230CrVMo 14 9	2.3	14	9	1, formerly CPM-420-V

WL-34, ELMAX, CPM-S30-V and CPM-S90-V are made with powdered metal.

to higher wear of tools and grinding bands. These factors make a knife made of this superior material correspondingly more expensive.

The Effects of the Elements in Steel

Why is iron alloyed anyway? Steel needs carbon because iron can be hardened in the presence of carbon.

Steels alloyed with chromium, vanadium, nickel, cobalt or tantalum decisively improve the properties of the steel.

Carbon makes the hardness possible and forms carbides with iron and the other elements. Carbides are extremely hard carbon compounds.

Chromium increases the steel's resistance to corrosion. With 13% or more chromium content, steel is rust-resistant. Chromium increased the hardness and resistance to dulling.

Vanadium increases the steel's firmness and resistance to dulling, as do tantalum, nickel, molybdenum and tungsten.

Steel Designations

From the previous section, the user can see how important knowledge of the types of steel is when one buys a knife.

Factory-made knives often are simply marked "rust-free" or "stainless" on the blade. Sometimes one also finds the marking "440." These are not much help. Any steel with a certain percentage of chromium in its alloy is rust-free. Being in the 440 family also does not say much, since 440A, 440B and 440C differ considerably in their composition, which shows up in their performance and, not least, in their prices.

In knives of high value, one finds more precise steel designations. It may be the DIN number, such as *X105CrMo 17 4*, or the one from the Steel Key, which represents a data bank that describes all existing steels by their properties, uses and heat-treating requirements, in terms of hardness and temper.

From the DIN designation one can determine the composition of the steel. In the example above, the X indicates that it is a highly alloyed steel with more than 5% of alloying metals added to the iron. The number after the X indicates the carbon content. Divided by 100, it gives the carbon percentage. In our case, 105 = 1.05%. The letters that follow indicate the main alloying metals, here Cr for chromium and Mo for molybdenum. The following numbers show the percentages of the alloying elements in order, here 17% chromium and 4% molybdenum.

A crude rule of thumb is that the higher the carbon content, the numbers and percentages of the added elements are, the more valuable the steel is.

Thus the DIN designation gives information on important characteristics of the steel in question.

Some manufacturers use the Steel Key number to give information on the type of steel. For example, **1.4125** stands for 440° Celsius.

The material number tells the layman nothing and the specialist little. Here one must take the trouble to look in the Steel Key. Interested parties can buy the book at a knife shop.

In our case, the specialist looks at the **1**, which tells him that it is an iron material. The **4** stands for acid- and rust-resistance (thus a chrome steel), and the **1** after the 4 shows that molybdenum is present in the alloy. The last two digits are just serial numbers.

Properties of Steels in use:

440C	High corrosion-resistance
ATS34	High wear-resistance
Damascene	High corrosion- and wear-resistance, fine appearance
RWL34	Like ATS34, can be hardened more because of higher breakage resistance.

Besides the chemical properties of the steel, meaning its composition, the heat treatment is of decisive importance.

With optimal heat treatment, the specialist can conjure a blade with superior properties out of a steel that is mediocre in terms of its composition. Conversely, a simple factory treatment degrades an expensive super-alloy into a blade with mediocre properties.

Several factors play a role in heat treatment: Hardening temperature, duration at that temperature range, quenching medium (air, oil, water), temperature of the medium, additions to the oil or water, tempering temperature and duration, frequency of tempering, deep-cooling treatment in liquid nitrogen, etc. The "high school of heat treatment" is pure handwork, calling for much experience and time. Thus it cannot be done by most cutlery-producing factories, which absolutely should not mean that their products are thus of low value. The "high school of heat treatment," though, requires the individual specialist, which is naturally reflected in the price of the knife.

One of the most important properties of a blade is its hardness. The blade should not be so hard that it breaks easily, but should be hard enough to hold the sharpening, to maintain its sharpness and cutting ability. By *hardness* is meant the resistance that a material applies to resist another, harder material. The hardness of tool steel is measured in *Rockwell,* abbreviated HRC. The Rockwell hardness should be between 56 and 62 HRC for knives, depending on their type of use. This means the higher the number, the greater the hardness. The diamond, the hardest material that exists, has a Rockwell hardness of 100.

For hardness testing, a diamond wedge is pressed into the tool and its depth of penetration is measured. A scale then shows the Rockwell hardness. The hardness is influenced by the heat treatment, especially the tempering. The tempering temperature and duration determine the hardness of the steel in use.

But first the steel must attain its final hardness. Highly alloyed tool steel is brought to its hardening temperature in a vacuum. The steel procedure declares this temperature. The piece is heated in a vacuum or inert gas, usually argon, as it would have a chemical reaction on its surface under the influence of oxygen. The burning off of so-called *dross* would take place. The surface would thus be influenced negatively, and would have to be reworked after hardening.

After the steel has reached the prescribed temperature, it is cooled in a hardening medium. One differentiates among oil, air, and water media. The simpler steels, such as carbon steel, are quenched in water. Highly alloyed steels need gentler media such as oil or compressed air. After quenching, the steel is too hard to be used. It would break easily under pressure. As already noted, tempering is the right means of attaining the desired hardness for use. The steel is heated again, but to a considerably lower temperature than in hardening, and then cooled again. In temper-ing, the surface of the steel changes color, as a thin layer of oxide forms. The color differs according to the thickness, which is related to the temperature. One can compare this in something like oil on water.

The tempering colors show to which temperature the steel was exposed. From this, conclusions can be drawn about the hardness, if one knows the temperature range applicable to the type of special steel in conjunction with the hardness.

Example:

A blade made of C90 carbon steel should be tempered to a hardness of 58 HRC. From information from the maker or dealer, it is known that this C90 attains its 58 HRC at some 250° C. A look at the table with the tempering colors shows that 250° equals a brown-red color. Thus the blade is heated until it is colored brown-red and then cooled.

Reading this from the tempering colors is of special interest if no hardening oven with a readable temperature scale is available, or if it cannot be used, perhaps in partial hardening.

Partial hardening means making the cutting edge of a knife very hard while the rest of the blade remains softer, thus more flexible and less likely to break.

This can be done as follows: The blade is tempered to a relatively hard degree, say 60 HRC. Then the knifemaker places it in a water bath that covers only the cutting edge. Then he warms the back of the blade with the flame of a welding device until the color shows the desired hardness is attained.

Tempering Colors for Carbon Steels

White-yellow	200° C	Violet	280° C
Straw yellow	220° C	Dark blue	290° C
Golden yellow	230° C	Med. blue	300° C
Yellow-brown	240° C	Light blue	320° C
Brown-red	250° C	Blue-gray	340° C
Red	260° C	Gray	360° C
Purple-red	270° C		

For highly alloyed steels, the temperature range moves upward.

Example of heat treatment prescription for popular 440C knife steel:

Forging temp.	900-1100° C
Hardening temp.	1000-1050° C
Hardening medium	Oil
Tempering temp.	100-300° C, HRC 57-60°

The flexibility of the steel can be improved further by deep-cooling in liquid nitrogen at about –60° C.

The discovery of iron hardening was probably the most important step in the history of steel production. The first smiths who made this important discovery probably protected their discovery carefully. It provided decisive advantages for making hardened tools or weapons.

In early cultures, smiths were highly esteemed, and magic powers were even attributed to them.

When buying a knife from a knifemaker, a customer should give decisive importance to the aspects of steel quality and the properties of the blade. It may be that the knife is meant only for the showcase and will never be put to practical use. But even for strictly collectors' knives, the maker will surely choose a steel of the best quality. It simply makes no sense to put high degrees of work, skill and materials into a knife but skimp on the steel.

Damascus Steel

Damascus Steel Over the Years

Fred Schmalz

The smith of prehistoric times was the most important handworker. For only he could turn the so-called *bloom* that was obtained in a forge from iron ore and charcoal into iron and steel.

No matter where the smith lived, in Europe, Asia or Africa, the procedure was the same. In the outer part of the bloom, the material

Fred Schmalz

was comparatively soft; in the inner area it was rich in carbon and hard.

The Celts of the Latene era (6th to 5th century B.C.) already knew how to produce Damascus steel from these materials. They also valued the characteristics that Damascus steel had to offer.
Generations of smiths refined the technology of welded steel (Damascus or Damascene steel). We continue to improve the steel, by giving Damascus steel more enduring sharpness, sturdiness, resistance to corrosion, elegance and purity. We have it easier, for we can also choose from the many steels that the steel industry offers us.

Here it is like cooking. Only the best ingredients provide a good menu. The right choice of steels, knowledge of their chemical composition, expert workmanship and the resulting heat treatment are prerequisites for a good Damascus steel. Thus it is possible to produce a welded steel that stands up to comparison with all previous knife steels. The quality of the steel gives it the elegance and uniqueness that a normal steel does not have to offer.

Blades of Damascus steel never were or are produced in large quantities. They are individual pieces that can be compared to fingerprints in terms of their structure. The smith who has produced the Damascus is recognizable in the steel, for each one has a different way of forming the iron in the fire, giving it his personal stamp. Sharpness, lasting value, and elegance: Damascus steels and knives that are handmade according to customers' wishes are witnesses of a living handcrafting art.

As hard as it sometimes is, I am always happy to be a handcrafting smith.

Fred Schmalz

Production of Damascus and Damascene Types

It is not easy to turn away from the fascination of Damascus steel. This noble material reflects ancient tradition and handcrafting art.

The Greek historian Herodotus (ca. 484-ca. 425 B.C.) once said that "war is the father of all things." This is surely true of the invention of Damascus steel. At that time there were two types of iron: hard cast iron with a carbon content of over 1.5%, which could not be wrought, and soft wrought iron. Both types were only conditionally suitable for swords. Cast iron broke quickly and wrought iron bent. Damascus steel united the properties of both types in an ideal manner. It combined hardness and elasticity. The owner of a Damascus sword had a weapon that gave him clear advantages in a swordfight against an opponent who lacked a Damascus sword.

But how did the so-called welded steels originate?

They originated at the place which has served mankind for millennia: the smith's fire. Naturally, the present-day material no longer comes from the forge where our forebears melted their raw iron, although there are still enthusiasts today who make iron by this ancient method. Suitable types of steel are available in the trade. The steels should be as pure as possible, which positively influences their workability. But one can also find suitable steels on the scrap heap, old coil springs, or shafts, for example.

Two and sometimes more types of steel are arranged alternately in a co-called package. The dimensions of the steel plates can be stated as 20 to 30 mm wide and 80 to 100 mm long. The number of steel plates is usually odd, seven or nine. They produce a total thickness of 30 to 50 mm. The pieces

Smith Juergen Rosinski works a steel package into Damascus steel.

have to be metallically plain, or they will not weld with each other. The package is held together by being wrapped in heat-resistant cord. One can also fix the plates by welding them together at their two ends.

The smith often makes the last piece longer, so it can serve as a handle.

The package is brought up to temperature in the forge fire. The right temperature is shortly before the melting point. Even for experienced smiths, finding the right temperature can be very tricky. If the steel gets too hot, it burns up. That means that the carbon in the steel will burn and the steel will thus become unusable. If the temperature is too low, the welding does not succeed. It is also important that the whole package has the same temperature. It requires some experience to recognize the right temperature by the glowing color. This is probably also a reason why the forge in the smithy is situated in a dark area, and thus made its way into the mystic, secret realm earlier. The time that the steel spends in the fire is also important. If it takes too long, material burns off and is lost. Iron was once an expensive raw material. Thus the loss was to be kept as little as possible. One estimated the time in the fire by reciting rhymes and verses. Thus one could deter-

Juergen Rosinski checks the welded package.

DAMASCUS STEEL

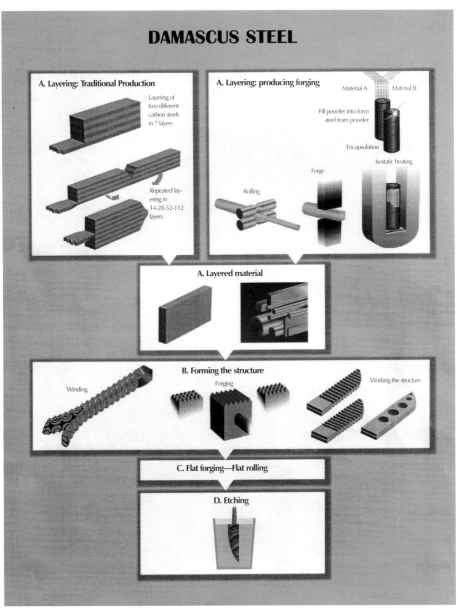

A. Layering: Traditional Production

Layering of two different carbon steels in 7 layers

Repeated layering in 14-28-52-112 layers

A. Layering: producing forging

Material A   Material B

Fill powder into form steel from powder

Encapsulation

Isostatic heating

Forge

Rolling

A. Layered material

B. Forming the structure

Winding

Forging

Working the structure

C. Flat forging—Flat rolling

D. Etching

A simplified view of the formation of Damascus steel.
With the friendly cooperation of Damasteel AB.

mine the time quite exactly without using a clock. Thus it is not surprising that the smith was surrounded by an aura of mystery.

One need only imagine a mighty, soot-blackened man muttering to himself in a dark corner while the steel glows in the fire.

If the steel has a yellowish-white color, which indicates the right temperature, the first and most important fire-welding can begin. Speed is required in welding, since the steel welds only in a very limited temperature range.

The steel should also be exposed as little as possible to the oxygen in the air, since the resulting layer of oxide hinders the welding. To avoid it, the smith uses a *flux.* Quartz sand, the so-called *welding sand,* was used in the past. Today Borax is used. The flux melts when it is strewn on the hot steel, envelops it and thus prevents the formation of oxide. The flux penetrates into the interstices by capillary action and prevents them from burning.

Now the package must be moved quickly to the anvil, and the smith hammers it together with even strokes, beginning on one side. Thus flux and impurities are driven out the other side and the steel plates are welded together. This takes place under a heavy rain of sparks. If everything works, a package of layered Damascus results. Now, if desired, it can be forged further, folded and welded again, in order to increase the number of layers.

After the desired number of layers is attained, the pattern can be made. This is done by twisting (torsion Damascus), stamping, or milling.

The stamped and milled patterns appear later on the surface, since the steel is forged flat again after this working, and thus the layers cut below come to the surface.

In Damascus steel, qualities such as cutting ability, corrosion-resistance, color contrast, behavior when etched, etc., depend very much on the choice of steel types, which the smith often keeps a secret.

As those who love this material say, Damascus has a soul.

The Damascus that is made in the smith's fire is not rust-free, since chrome steels are not suitable for the traditional type of fire-welding, and a chromium content of over 13% is required for rust-free steel.

But traditional Damascus can be sharpened well and thus is in no way inferior to the so-called *monosteel.*

The typical Damascus pattern is formed by etching with sulfuric acid or iron trichloride. The acid attacks the welded steel types in different ways, so that one can recognize the layers and thus the patterns.

The large rose, stamped above and ground below.

Power-metal Damascus, deeply etched.

One type of steel remains lighter, which is caused by a higher nickel content in the steel; the other becomes darker. If the Damascus remains in the acid longer, a kind of relief forms, since the "weaker" steel is removed faster.

There are many types, patterns and combinations of Damascus steel. We shall have a look at the most important ones here. Damascus can be divided into three basic categories: layered, torsion, and mosaic Damascus.

Layered Damascus: These include all types in which the steel layers are parallel to the blade. Simple utilitarian knives have between 40 and 120 layers, But there can be many more. There are Japanese sword blades with up to two million layers.

In the past, attempts were made to forge the steel as finely as possible for the sake of better cutting. But since fine Damascus can scarcely be recognized with the naked eye, the number of layers is limited now. It should be recognizable that the steel is Damascus. A number of layers up to 1000 is still quite possible. In working the blade, a kind of high-line relief is formed, which

makes the blade contour visible as if on a map.

Wild Damascus: As the name suggests, the pattern of this Damascus is not orderly, thus wild. Here specific patterns, such as are formed in most other types of Damascus, are not created. The patterns are formed by chance through irregular treatment with the smith's hammer. This Damascus is fittingly called *Random Damascus* in the USA.

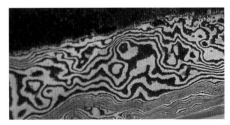

Wild Damascus knife by Murat Klein.

Wild Damascus details.

Large and Small Rose: This Damascus is formed by stamping layered Damascus. The smith presses stamps made of tool steel into the hot steel. Thus the positions of the individual layers are somewhat changed. In the ensuing grinding, the stamped-in patterns appear on the surface. It is important that the patterns be pressed in deeply, since they will otherwise disappear in the later working. Because of their soft, rounded shapes, these patterns are not suitable for all types of knives. But that, like so much, is a matter of taste.

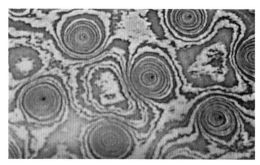

Close-up of the small rose pattern on a knife by Joe Poehler.

Small rose, knife by Joe Poehler.

Japanese Damascus: This layered Damascus is so delicate that its individual layers usually can no longer be seen with the naked eye. Up to two million layers seem like an awful lot, but that is not so difficult. If you start with a steel packet of eight layers, after folding it eight times you have theoretically 2048 layers. One must keep in mind that losses occur in the process. The etching of Japanese Damascus is not common. A special polish makes the steel structure come out. As noted, this fine steel does not stand out for its Damascus structure. The blade rather shows a hardness line, the so-called *Hamon*. To create this line, the blade is covered with a special clay mix up to its cutting edge. Only the uncovered parts take part in the hardening. This procedure, when used on swords, has the advantage of letting the sword itself remain flexible, with only the cutting edge hard and somewhat brittle. Thus the danger of breaking is reduced.

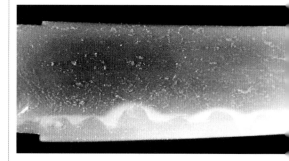

Details of a Japanese sword blade (Katana). The hardness line can be seen clearly.

Banded Damascus: The starting material for banded Damascus is, again, layered Damascus that is stamped at regular intervals vertically to the axis of the blade. Similarly to rose Damascus, further working brings out the characteristic banded pattern. Here too, sufficiently deep stamping is important, so that the pattern remains after the working.

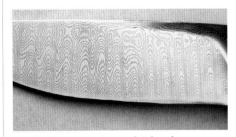

Banded Damascus by Fred Schmalz.

Nickel Damascus: In this layered Damascus, Reinnicke plates are added to the welding package to heighten the contrast effect. This is not unproblematic, though, since nickel cannot be hardened, thus it offers no cutting performance. As an alloying element, nickel gives the advantage of making the steel more resistant to etching and makes polished steel brighter. But not everything that shines also cuts well. If a thin layer of nickel is in the cutting area, it will surely wear unevenly. Thus it is advantageous to build up the Damascus deliberately. In the cross-section of the blade, the central area remains without nickel, with contrasting material containing nickel to the left and right.

Torsion Damascus: In the production of torsion Damascus, layered steel of 7 to 23 layers in rod form is forged and twisted in a glowing condition. The rods, twisted alternately to the left and right, are then welded together. But a single twisted rod can also be forged. This type of Damascus, though, requires more work, since the smith must produce a good layered Damascus as a final product. While twisting, he must be sure that the steel does not tear, especially if he tries to make too many twists. Blades made of several twisted rods require a high degree of work, which also influences their price.

Nickel Damascus knife by
Ernst G. Siebeneicher-Hellwig.

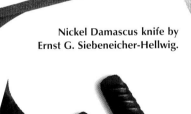

Torsion Damascus construction
made by Johannes Ebner.

27

Knife by Franz Hutzler with torsion Damascus blade by Juergen Ruehl.

Turkish Damascus: When building up 6 or more strands, one speaks of Turkish Damascus. This Damascus is very laborious to create and thus ranks among the most expensive types of Damascus. Whoever orders a Turkish Damascus knife from a smith must expect a long waiting time. In that time he can save up the money that is needed for a purchase of this kind.

A fully integral knife by Stefan Steigerwald, made of Turkish Damascus by Markus Balbach.

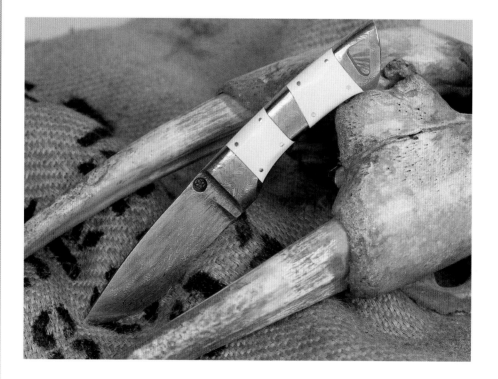

Torsion Damascus with cutting ridge: To improve the cutting performance of torsion Damascus knives, a cutting ridge of mono-steel or fine Damascus is forged. It not only looks good, but is also useful. The cutting ridge of a finely forged layered Damascus is more homogeneous. High-value steels can also be selected for the cutting ridge, which can cause problems in twisting. Here one should strive for a nice parallel line between the cutting ridge and first twisted track.

Details of torsion Damascus with a cutting ridge.

Torsion Damascus with cutting ridge. Damascus by Guido Wilbert, knife by Stefan Steigerwald.

.

Chainsaw and Wire Damascus: For purists, these forms of Damascus represent a controversial special form. Old chains from chainsaws or wires of hardenable steel are forged as raw pieces. Motorcycle chains have also been used, which perhaps makes many a biker's heart beat faster. The results are very much worth seeing, but the cutting performance is less spectacular, since the basic material was not made for knife production.

Chainsaw Damascus knife by Christian Deminie.

Mosaic Damascus: Here pictures and patterns from various steels are combined. Making this product is scarcely possible any more with the old hammer-and-anvil method. High-pressure presses are used, since they turn out uniform results. The patterns are usually made up of rectangular profiles, since they can be combined better to guarantee optimal welding. When the bundle is welded, layers of it are cut off. These mosaic plates, some 25 x 30 mm, are suitable for bolsters or end pieces. If one wants to make a blade, these plates must be lined up and welded.

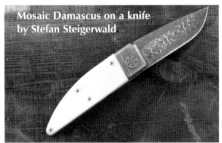

Mosaic Damascus on a knife by Stefan Steigerwald

Mosaic Damascus on a knife by Juergen Ruehl.

Meteorite Damascus: This exotic Damascus type consists of fire-welded carbon steel and pieces of iron meteorites. The layers that are raised after etching are the meteorite inlays. With their higher nickel content, they are less attacked by the acid and also remain brighter. The Malay *Kris,* (a dagger, often with a flamed blade) is well known and regarded as sacred. Meteorite iron was used in their production.

One cannot see whether a blade was made of meteorite iron. Meteorite iron is better used a few centimeters farther back, as bolster material or handle inlays—etched or with a melted crust, such as results when the heavenly bodies enter the earth's atmosphere.

Meteorite Damascus knife by Markus Bahlbach.

Meteorite Damascus details.

RUST-FREE DAMASCUS:
1. Forged Damascus: Steels with high proportions of chromium cannot be fire-welded easily. But there are tricks. The problem is that chromium, when heated in conjunction with oxygen, instantly forms an oxide layer. The chromium oxide prevents the welding of the steel layers. The few smiths who master the making of rust-free Damascus are able to limit the oxygen while welding.

This Damascus steel is very corrosion-resistant, although it does not attain the cutting ability of the Damascus made by powder metallurgy. Yet it offers an interesting alternative to the carbon Damascus steel of equal cutting ability. The fact that only a few smiths master the production of rust-free Damascus steel makes it more valuable.

Resistance to corrosion is a strong argument for this Damascus. Not every buyer of an elaborately made Damascus knife puts it in a showcase, but will also want to use it, perhaps to cut corrosive materials like acid fruit or fat meat.

2. Powder-Metallurgic Damascus: A Swe-

Rust-free Damascus by Fritz Schneider, knife by Klaus Papke.

dish firm has developed a process to make PM Damascus. The product is called *Damasteel®*. This steel, made by the most elaborate process, is winning more and more popularity.

In powder metallurgy, alloy elements can also be included in concentrations which the conve1

most stringent requirements. The starting material is a very fine metal powder. It is formed when molten metal is pressed through fine nozzles in a vacuum or under inert gas.

The individual layers are formed by a clever process by which the various metal powders are treated. The powder layers are then baked fast to each other in a doughy state under high pressure and heat. Then comes the further formation, as with "normal" Damascus. Patterns are stamped and rods are twisted. The further working to form the blade is problem-free.

Sharpness retention and rust-resistance are very good, thanks to the good and richly added "additions." PM Damascus has the property of increasing its hardness when tempered at 500° C. This quality can be utilized to color *Damasteel* by the effect of heat. The smith heats the blade to 500° C after hardening and tempering, and the blade turns bluish-red. It looks very unusual. A blade made of conventional steel would lose too much hardness at 500° C.

Powder-metal Damascus blades in various patterns.

Deeply etched powder-metal Damascus; knife by Ernst G. Siebeneicher-Hellwig.

Powder-metal Damascus, knife by Stefan Steigerwald.

nfortunately, such tempering colors generally do not last long. It is usually no longer possible to repeat the heat treatment of the finished knife afterward. Thus this coloring is more suitable for showcase knives.

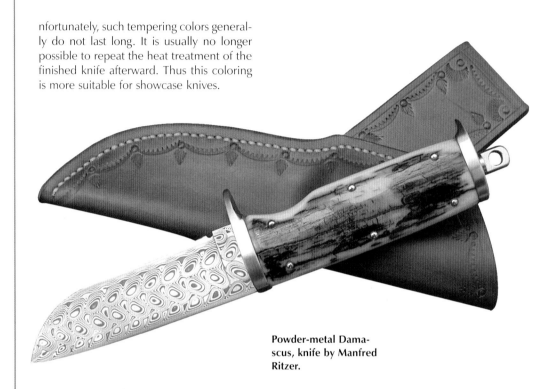

Powder-metal Damascus, knife by Manfred Ritzer.

Melted Damascus: A special type of Damascus is the *Wootz Steel.* Wootz is not forged but rather a cast Damascus. That means that the various steels are not forged together but melted together. The additives—various types of ore and charcoal—are heated to the melting point in a crucible.

Detail of a Wootz steel dagger.

The dagger shown below is a so-called *Djambija*, some 200 years old, from the Indo-Persian area. The original material for the blade was the so-called *Wootzking*, which is the casting cake into which it came out of the crucible. The Wootzking was forged into a blade. The blade was smoothed and whetted with rubies fitted into special holders, then brought to a high polish with a hardened Wootz-steel polishing iron, and finally treated with plant juices to bring out the *Jauhar*, the Wootz drawing.

Wootz steel dagger with casting cake, loaned by Dahn A. Olbricht.

The Problem of Choice

The question of which type of Damascus steel to choose depends on many points of view and, ultimately, on taste.

The powder-metallurgical Damascus charms with its excellent cutting performance and high resistance to rust.

The traditional Damsacus has the charm of authenticity. It can be sharpened well, but gets tarnished and rusts easily.

Materials for Fittings

The material between the blade and handle of a *Steckangel* knife is called the *fitting material*. On *full-tang* knives, on the other hand, fittings are attached at the same places on the right and left, or fitted in slit form as hand protectors.

The means and methods of fitting include, among others, riveting, screwing, swallow-tail fitting, soldering, gluing and other types. The knifemaker should choose fitting material that is sturdy and easy to work, resistant to corrosion, tarnishing, scratching, etc.

The fittings of high-quality knives gain more and more significance, above and beyond their pure functionality, be it through the use of fine materials, artistic engraving or extravagant formation.

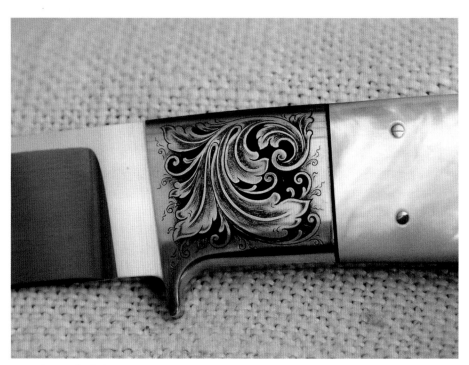

Engraving on the bolster.

Bolster and Guard Elements

A fully integral knife by Dietmar Kressler. The bolsters and butt are made from the metal.

Most often, knifemakers used such metals as stainless steel, bras, copper, German silver, aluminum, titanium and bronze. Precious metals such as silver and gold are found more rarely, as opposed to Mokume (see below), anodized titanium or meteoric iron. The latter are found mainly in folding knives.

The most commonly used materials will be described below.

Brass: This copper-zinc alloy can be worked well, but that's really its only good point. Brass tarnishes very quickly and can, for example, form poisonous verdigris in leather sheaths. Brass is simple to work, and a great variety of profiles can be used. The knifemaker thus needs to devote only a small amount of work to shaping.

Copper: There are hard and soft types of copper. Copper is often used for somewhat "sturdier" knives, to emphasize their character. Only with a noble patina does it really look good. When polished, it does not keep its glow very long.

Besides being treated with *potassium sulfide*, there are other means of coloring copper in various tones. The Japanese are known for their artistic coloring techniques. One needs sharp tools to work it, for copper likes to smear, which results in messy surfaces.

Bronze: There are various bronzes. The classic tin bronze looks best, showing a warm reddish golden tone after a short time. One can patinize the surface (color it chemically) or temper it (color it thermally). Tin bronze can be worked well.

Aluminum: It is best to choose medium-hard or hard aluminum alloys that do not smear much when being worked. Aluminum is very light, but unfortunately tarnishes over time and is easily scratched. The resistance of the surface can be much improved by eloxying. In addition, an extensive array of colors can be had, After eloxying, the parts can no longer be worked, as the layer would be damaged and come off. Thus it is best to attach finished aluminum parts to the knife with screws.

Stainless Steel: In terms of its optical qualities, stainless steel would be very good for fittings. Unfortunately, it is tough and requires a lot of work and tool use. The polished surface is still easy to scratch. Thus it is better to fall back on hardenable stainless steel (such as a knife steel). Naturally, it must be hardened; otherwise it is not rust-free. It is recommended that one work ahead as far as possible, as it can and should only be worked with grinding tools afterward.

Titanium: Titanium is, in terms of specific weight, only half as heavy as steel, and looks very impressive. Pure titanium is softer and thus easier to work than titanium alloys, most of which come from aerospace technology. Titanium is not good at releasing heat—this is also the reason why it

feels so pleasantly warm. Because of its poor head conduction, the knifemaker must consider moderate cutting speeds and good cooling when working it. Titanium can be colored anodically (with electricity and electrolytes) and thermally (by heating).

Precious Metals: Gold and silver are quite rarely used as fitting materials. One reason is their cost, the other is their properties. These metals are simply too soft for use as fittings.

Mokume: *Mokume gane* (Japanese, meaning more or less "wood") is a very old development from Japan. The material, made of several metals, has long been used for containers and for fittings of swords and daggers.

In the making of mokume, various bright metals like brass, copper and German silver, as well as precious metals like silver and gold, are firmly combined.

Mokume.

Knife by Ernst G. Siebeneicher-Hellwig, with mokume bolsters and decorative rivets.

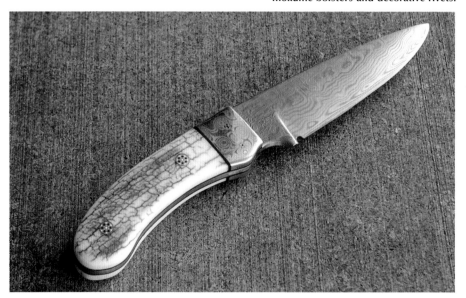

In technical terms, the process is called *diffusion combining*. Thin sheets of the metals are placed on each other. The resulting pile is heated until the metals begin to become doughy. Under pressure, the surfaces of the metals are permanently bound to each other. This process is called diffusion because atoms of the adjoining alloys move into each other at the junctures—in German, *diffundieren*—and remain there. Thus new alloys arise in the border areas.

The nice thing about mokume is that in working it with files or grinders, the various layers are cut and become visible as patterns on the surface.

Because of the optical appearance as well as the formative process, mokume can be compared with Damascus steel.

The choice of fitting materials strongly influences the usable value and appearance of a knife. They need not always be metal. Other materials such as wood, horn, ivory or plastic also find their fans. Their use–like everything in knifemaking–is basically dependent on design and function. Would it not be a good idea to fit a survival knife with a guard piece of magnesium that could be heated if necessary?

Meteorite Iron: Heavy bolsters of meteorite iron (not rust-free!) usually excite the viewer. They have the mythical charm of the "extraterrestrial." Who would not like to have a piece of iron that, eons ago, was flung into space by an exploding supernova and landed on earth as a meteorite after traveling many million years?

Pieces of meteorite iron.

Meteorite iron is only recognizable as such after etching, which brings out the so-called *Widmanstaetten figures.*

These unique, very decorative patterns occur only in meteorites, and then only in certain types. They are formed by the extremely long cooling times in the cores of former stars or planets.

The patterns are typical of the group of *octahedrites* among the iron meteorites. In this group are the 27-ton *Sikhote-Alin* that landed in Russia in 1938, the 21-ton *Gibeon* that landed in Namibia about a million years ago, and the 58-ton *Cape York* that fell on Greenland in 1894. Naturally, there are other iron meteorites. But since little material is available, it is correspondingly expensive. Meteorite iron has increased much in value in recent years.

If one wants to etch meteorite iron to bring out the attractive figures, one must grind the material to at least 1200 grain and polish it carefully. This should be done very carefully, so as not to overheat the material. Many meteorites have fine cracks that enlarge when heated and can even cause breakage.

After polishing, degreasing is done with alcohol, spirits, or acetone. Etching is done in an acid bath. Nitol has proved itself here. It consists of 2% concentrated saltpeter acid by weight in 95% ethyl alcohol. The metal remains in the bath for several minutes and must be checked frequently until one is satisfied with the results. Personal taste is decisive here, as when etching Damascus.

Now the piece is thoroughly washed and dried. Then it is placed in an ethyl alcohol bath for two or three days.

In the handle area in particular, meteorite iron rusts easily from hand sweat. But not every meteorite rusts equally quickly.

There are also those that scarcely rust. Others, though, "bloom" again and again. This depends on the surroundings in which the meteor was placed. Chlorine soils encourage later rust formation.

The knifemaker must take this risk when buying meteorite iron. One cannot hold the seller responsible. Just treat the material frequently with rust remover.

The so-called Widmanstaetten figures come out when the surface of the meteorite iron is etched. They are caused by layers of nickel-poor and rich iron (bars, bands and fillings).

Collectors of meteorite iron coat their good pieces with clear lacquer, which is not recommended for knife parts.

Since the material cannot be worked after etching without spoiling the pattern, it makes sense to attach bolsters of meteorite iron to the handle with screws, work them, unscrew them, etch them and then screw them on again.

Rivets

The best types of rivets are rods. All the bright metals, such as brass, copper, bronze and German silver can be used, plus stainless steel, aluminum, and even precious metals.

Mosaic pins are an especially charming variant.

When they are made, metal tubes are filled with colored epoxy resins, usually red, white or blue. Then rods or small tubes are added and arranged in patterns. After the resin hardens, one has a solid piece of rivet rod, which reveals a nice pattern in its final working.

The attachment of a mosaic pin is quite simple. First one glues the two halves of the handle and bores 3-mm holes at the desired places. These holes are now bored out from both sides to the diameter of the mosaic pin (usually 6 mm). It is best to do this with a countersink bit, but a drill can also be used. Now an M-3 bolt is screwed in with a nut. One must be careful that the screw head is at least 2 mm below the surface of the handle. One fills in this difference with a slice of the mosaic pin. Then it is ground down carefully.

Mosaic rivets and mokume bolsters.

Cutlery Rivets: As the name implies, these rivets are used in cutlery, usually kitchen knives. They are also found in American knives form pioneer times or their reproductions.* This is not surprising, since many "Wild West" knives go back to kitchen or butcher knives. The two-piece rivets hold by being pressed together. The not very high heads thus press into the handle material. In our knives with hard, high-pried handle wood, this could cause cracking. Then too, they look rather cheap.

Screw Rivets: They are based on the principle of the threaded shaft or bolt and nut.

Threading offers the convenience of very quick assembly, especially when the screwed pieces are also glued together.

Since bolt heads and nuts must be countersunk, it is necessary to bore countersink holes. Suitable bits can be had in the tool and material trade, but a typical spiral drill also does the job.

For the type of screw rivet that includes a threaded shaft and two nuts, the choice of various metals for the rods and nuts can form a so-called *bull's-eye effect*, a specialty of old master Bob Loveless (see picture on page 61).

From left to right, cutlery rivets, screw rivets and countersink.

* The fine work by Matthias Recktenwald, *Bowie Knives—An American Myth,* is recommended. Stuttgart, Motorbuch Verlag, 2003.

Handle Materials

Wood

While researching for this book, the authors noted the great variety of woods that are used in the trade. Some 4000 of the world's approximately 27,000 types of wood can be used in handcrafting. Naturally, not all of the 4000 are suitable for knifemaking.

A good knife stands out, among other things, through neat, even transitions from the handle material to the metal parts. Thus only stable, sturdy wood is suitable for knifemaking.

The newcomer will feel overwhelmed by the variety of colors and grain patterns of the available woods, and may want to experiment. To avoid later disappointment—such as if a knife made with much care does not look good—the choice of wood should be made carefully.

Every wood, no matter how long it has been aged, will change its size and shape because of temperature and moisture changes. Long seasoning of the wood is very important. Only absolutely dry wood may be used, to be safe from later surprises. To attach the wood firmly to the knife, the knifemaker can do several things: gluing, screwing, riveting, cutting dovetails. But wood can develop very great strength. The ancient Egyptians once broke stone out of their quarries by using swelling wooden wedges.

The great variety of types will be limited by usability. Thus only 30 to 50 types of wood suitable for knifemaking are available in the trade. We shall look at these below. Wood that stands out for its stability is very popular. Among them are desert ironwood, grenadil, ebony, and boxwood. The knifemaker can reduce the absorption of moisture and the resulting problems by treating the wood surface. Wax, shellac, and linseed oil products can be used, as well as synthetic paint. But these products do not penetrate completely into the wood, being absorbed to only 3 to 5 mm. Thus it is not possible to guarantee a lastingly perfect bonding between wood and metal. To minimize the risk, here are a few suggestions:

- Use stable wood that will not shrink much.
- Do not let the wood get too hot when working it.
- Make sure of stable attachment to the handle (screws, rivets, glue, fitting).
- Use pore-filling, water-deflecting surface treatment.
- When gluing, be sure that the wood is well degreased. Some tropic woods have a large oil content which, experience shows, glue does not like.

Before we look at the individual types of wood, here are a few basics. There are various qualities of wood, from simple grain to extravagant. Naturally, this influences the price. Thus an especially nicely grained rootstock can cost many times more than a simple one.

The knives shown here were made with woods of standard to very good quality.

Rootwood is generally stronger than *stemwood*. This is based on the tasks of the various wood cells. Rootwood is made to absorb, store and pass on nutrients dissolved in water, while stemwood has conducting and stabilizing functions. Their resistance to shrinkage is thus different. A rule of thumb for native woods is that shrinkage (changing form because of moisture changes) adds up to 0.1% lengthwise, 10% tangentially in the direction of the annual rings, and 5% radially to the center of the trunk.

Tropical woods and slow-growing types have considerably better resistance to shrinkage.

UV rays (sunlight or halogen lamps) can cause unwanted color changes in originally colorful wood. The owner can protect against them by not exposing the knife constantly to bright sunshine or halogen light.

Wood dust can cause allergies. So do not inhale dust; wear a dust mask.

The picture shows the variety of natural colors in woods.
Knives by Ernst G. Siebeneicher-Hellwig.

Rootwood maple. Knife by Ernst G. Siebeneicher-Hellwig.

Root-grain Maple

WOOD TYPES AND THEIR PROPERTIES

Maple *Acer pseudoplanatus* (Planetree or Birdseye Maple)
Widespread in the Northern Hemisphere. Very little shrinkage, relatively hard and fine-pored. Can be livened up by colorful staining.
Tip: A "tiger-eye" look can be attained with modern stains. First a black (leather-colored) spirit stain is applied, then sanded until light spots appear again.

Then treat it with yellow-brown stain, seal well and polish.

Amaranth *Peltogyne venosa* (Purple Heart, Purplewood)
Northeastern South America. Very thick, even-grained wood. When first cut, it looks pale, which changes after a time. It can be sealed well and darkens under the influence of light.

Amaranth.

Amboina. Knife by Ernst G. Siebeneicher-Hellwig.

Amboina. Knife by Ernst G. Siebeneicher-Hellwig.

Amboina.

Amboina *Petrocarpus indicus*
Southeast Asia. Decorative but expensive rootwood. Can darken. Little shrinkage with good surface treatment. When worked, unexpected bad spots (cavities or enclosures) can appear. They can be filled with quick-drying glue mixed with sawdust. Since the wood is relatively soft, is should be sealed well. Fitting to the handle must be done carefully.

Bocote *Dalberniga nigra*
Mexico. Finely striped or grained veined wood, according to the cut. Very thick, oil-holding and weather-resistant. Should be well degreased before gluing.

Bocote.

Bocote. Knife by Eberhard Kaljumae.

Bruyere. Knife by Werner Schirmer.

Bruyere.

Bruyere *Callumna vulgaris*
Greece, Turkey. This wood is not only admirably suited for pipes, but is also very decorative on knives. It can be stained well to bring out more of the grain. Polishing with a shellac product is recommended. When well seasoned, it is stable and free of cavities. The wood is unfortunately not always available in top quality or large dimensions.

Bubinga *Guibontia tessmania* (African Rosewood)
West Africa. Very hard and polishable. Resists heat and coldness. Well suited for utilitarian knives. Great variations in the grain. *Bubinga* can be had with uniform coloring or with exciting grain, even optical tipping effect. The wood is easy to work.

Bubinga.

Bubinga. Knife by Andreas Has.

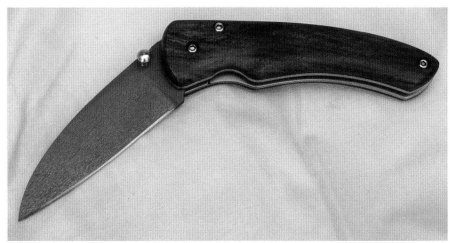

Boxwood. Knife by Siegfried Rinkes.

Boxwood

Boxwood *Buxus sempervirens*.
Southern Europe, North Africa, Asia Minor. Hard, thick, fine-grained wood with little shrinkage. When working it, be sure that the naturally light wood does not take up any dark (metal) grinding dust. It is best to seal it frequently.

Cocobolo.

Cocobolo *Dalberga retusa*
Northern Colombia. Very oily. Sealing should thus be eliminated. But Cocobolo is sensitive to light, so treatment with lacquer cannot hurt. Degrease the surface well before lacquering.
The sanding dust is *poisonous* and can set off strong allergic reactions. Here the rule applies, as in all dusty work: Wear a dust mask!

Cocobolo. Knife by Richard Spitzl.

Ebony. Knife by Johann Klemm.

Ebony.

African Ebony *Diospyros crassiflora*
Western and Eastern Africa, Madagascar. Very black, very stable, scarcely likely to crack after long seasoning. Since a grain is scarcely visible, it is often used for special shapes or Damascus knives. This avoids overloading the design.
One should use only very black ebony of this type. It is somewhat more costly, but the investment pays.

Macassar Ebony *Diospyros celebica*(Striped Ebony)
Southeast Asia, Indonesia. Decorative wood with similar characteristics to African ebony. Should be well sealed to

make it darker, but experiment with sealing first. The author has had good results with tung oil.

Macassar Ebony.

Macassar Ebony. Knife by Franz Hutzler with Damascus blade by Juergen Ruehl.

Fernambuk *Guilandia echinata* (Brazil Wood, Redwood)
South America. Stable, strikingly reddish-orange wood. Easy to work. One can use the sanding dust for homemade stains by mixing it with linseed oil and some linseed thinner (such as orange oil).

Fernambuk.

Fernambuk. Knife by Andreas Schweickert.

Grasswood *Xanthorrhoea australia*
Australia. Lightly grained, not noticeable. Many small dark spots on the outside. Available in the trade, so it should be mentioned here, but the authors feel it should be used only to ignite a charcoal grille or for knife sockets. Grasswood is too soft for utilitarian knives.

Grenadil. Knife by Franz Hutzler.

Grenadil.

Grenadil *Dalbergia melanoxylon* (African Blackwood, Mozambique Ebony)
Africa. Little shrinkage, very fine-pored and thick. With surface treatment with paint or oil, the not very noticeable grain can disappear completely. Grenadil is also used for African woodcarvings.

Jarrah *Eukalyptus marginata* (Yarrow Tree, Australian Mahogany)
Western Australia. Rootwood with many cavities. Color similar to Amboina. Open spots can be filled with artificial resin or other fillers, including colored types, but this is a matter of taste.

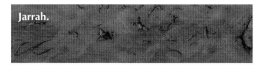

Jarrah.

Jarrah. Knife by Stefan Fromm.

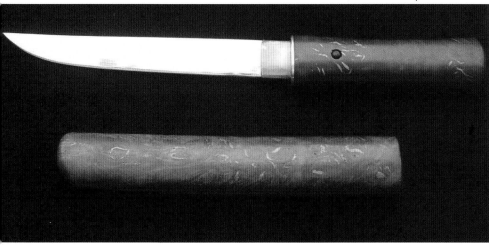

Grained Birch *Betula verrucosa*

Grained Birch

Finland, Russia. The traditional wood of the Nordic knife. Light and yet firm, since it grows slowly. Very decorative. Impregnate it well. Color can be changed by staining. Not completely free from shrinkage. The grain looks best when sealed with linseed products. Because of the shrinkage problem, it is best suited for Steckangel knives.

Nordic knives with grained birch handles.

Swamp Oak *Quercus spp.*

Swamp Oak.

Germany, Central Europe. The trees called "swamp oak" usually do not come from swamps, but from former swamps or watercourses, where they lasted for hundreds or thousands of years without air. Often they are trees from the edges of meadow groves and were undercut, felled by high waters, and finally covered with sediment. Depending on how long and where the oak trunk

Swamp Oak. Knife by Ernst G. Siebeneicher-Hellwig.

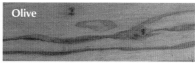

lay in the "swamp," the wood varies in firmness. That means one should test it (with a fingernail, but ask the dealer first) before buying. Firm dark pieces are rare, but lighter pieces also have their charm. Well suited for knifemaking. Clean the gluing surfaces well before gluing. There is a fascination in holding in your hand a piece of wood that sank in a swamp in early Germanic or Bronze Age times.

Olive *Olea europea*
Spain, Italy, France, Southwestern Europe. This wood is always busy. Sometimes it works, sometimes it splits. But it is very decorative.
Suitable for a curved-tang knife. Annoyance (shrinkage!) is programmed into its use as handle inlays of fully integral knives.

Knife with olive handle, by Erwin Schneller.

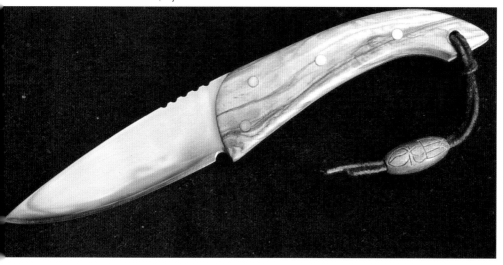

Padouk. Knife by Ernst G. Siebeneicher-Hellwig.

Padouk.

Padouk *Petrocarpus soyanxii* (Coralwood) West Africa, Well sealed and left in the shade, it more or less retains its shape and color. Working it is not a problem, but alas, somewhat "laborious."

Palmira *Borassus flabellifer* Africa, Australia. Inclined to crack. Tends to split when worked. The grain can disappear when sealed. It looks especially good from the front.

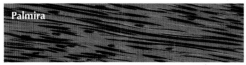

Palmira

Palmira. Knife by Klaus Papke.

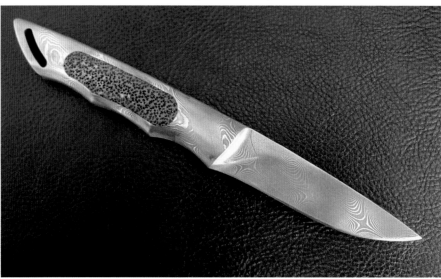

Palisander Honduras.

Palisander Honduras. Knife by Ernst G.
Siebeneicher-Hellwig.

Palisander *Dalbergia nigra, latfolia* (Rio
Santos or Amazon Palisander)
South Asia, Indonesia, East Indies, Brazil.
Very nice wood. Many color variations possible. Easy to work. The layman has a hard
time telling the different types of palisander
apart and should consult a specialist.

Pearlwood *Terminalia superba*
Many knifemakers think it looks very good,
since is shows very nice light reflections. But
it shrinks and is relatively soft. If you want,
stabilize or harden the surface with lacquer.

Pearlwood.

Pearlwood. Knife by Stefan Steigerwald.

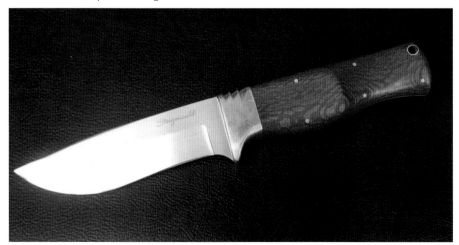

Pink Ivory. Knife by Ernst G. Siebeneicher-Hellwig.

Pink Ivory.

Pink Ivory *Berchemia zeyheri*
South Africa. Fine-pored rose-colored wood, rare. Very good qualities, little shrinkage, hard. Darkens and shows great color differences. Naturally, pink tones are a matter of taste, but along with other materials, Pink Ivory can look elegant.

Pockwood *Guaiacum officinale*
Central America, West Indies. Very oily, hard, and resistant wood. Very suitable for utilitarian knives. Darkens. Since is never really dries out, on account of the high oil content, it can crack after a long time. It was originally used to make water-wheel shafts and other waterworks.

Pockwood.

Pockwood. Knife by Andreas Schweikert.

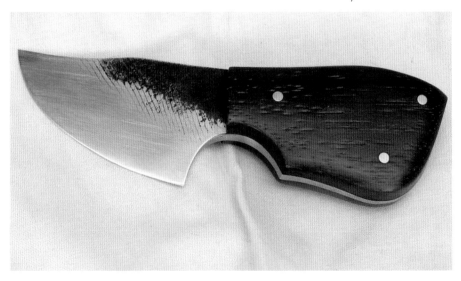

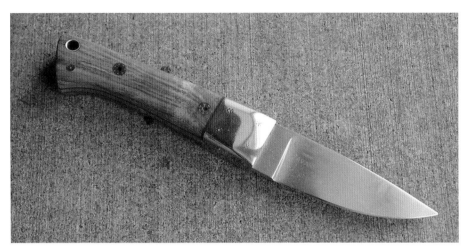

Rosewood.

Rosewood. Knife by Ernst G.
Siebeneicher-Hellwig.

Rosewood *Dalbergia varabilis* (Bahia Rosewood, Pinkwood, Paurosa)
Eastern Brazil. Very decorative, medium hard inclined to shrink, so seal it well.
Good evenly-patterned wood is hard to come by.

Guyana. Very nice wood, but can be problematic. Cracks can develop at rivets and holes. Shrinking and darkening are common. One can lessen the problems by careful working and seasoning. It is worthwhile! Still, one should not be disappointed if it splits. Usually a capable knifemaker can save something.

Snakewood *Piratinera guianensis*

Snakewood.

Snakewood. Knife by Fred Schmalz.

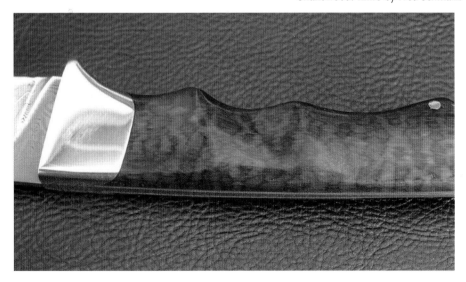

Arborvitae. Knife by Erwin Schneller.

Arborvitae.

Arborvitae *Arborvitae spp.* (Tree of Life, Thuja)
Algeria, Morocco. Very oily; tools and cleaning cloths will soon absorb it. Shrinks and darkens. Should be well seasoned before working and degreased before gluing. The wood smells pleasant.

Violetta *Dalbergia cearensis* (Kingswood)
South America. Nice wood but is inclined to split. Long seasoning and careful work pay off. After cutting, it looks somewhat pale, but it darkens again in air and light.

Violetta.

Violetta. Knife by Stefan Steigerwald.

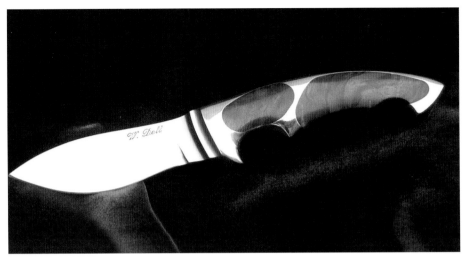

Walnut. Knife by Wolfgang Dell.

Walnut.

Walnut *Juglans vegia* (Burl)
Turkey. Fairly soft wood, better suited for gun butts than knives. In surface treatment, the wood can quickly become too dark. Best to try a test piece first.

Wenge *Millettia lauremntii*
West Africa. Fibrous but good to work. Appears rustic, stable. Avoid injuries; Wenge is *poisonous!*

Wenge.

Wenge. Knife by Ernst G. Siebeneicher-Hellwig.

Desert Ironwood *Olneya tesota*
Arizona, Mexico. Very old ironwood trees buried by desert sand have been found and cut. The most stable, least shrinking, but most expensive wood. Equally suitable for utilitarian and collectors' knives. Do not overheat when working it, as it may split. It should be smoothed very much, rather than polished with a swabbing disc, or the surface will become too wavy.

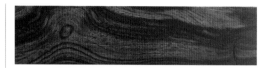

Desert Ironwood

Desert Ironwood. Knife by Ernst G. Siebeneicher-Hellwig.

Zebrano. Knife by Erwin Schneller.

Zebrano.

Zebrano *Microberlinia brazavillensis* (Zingana)
West Africa. Nice but not too firm wood. Caution with full-tang or fully integral knives that require exact fitting. Seal the surface well.

Zirkote *Codia sebestena*
Mexico. Very thick, interestingly grained wood, with a surface that looks like a map. Good qualities, simple to work. Very thick and fine-pored. The wood's beauty really comes out only when it is cut the right way.

Zirkote

Zirkote. Knife by Hans Geiger.

Stabilized Wood

Woods with low oil and resin contents can be *stabilized,* as the specialists say. The wood is thereby protected from shrinkage and swelling. To be stabilized, it is treated with acrylic resin in a vacuum.

The pores of the wood absorb the resin like a sponge, and after it hardens, the resin takes on the desired stabilizing effect. Addition of color allows charming effects to be created. Stabilized wood can be polished well.

The price of stabilized wood is, of course, a good deal higher, but the advantages are worth it.

Stabilized and colored wood, blade by Juergen Rosinski, knife by Ernst G. Siebeneicher-Hellwig.

Layered Wood

Layered wood is also known by the trade names of *Paccawood*® and *Dynawood*®.

It is made by laying thin plates of hardwood on each other, saturating them with artificial resin and hardening them under heat and pressure. The artificial resin content makes layered wood very stable. It does not shrink or bulge, and is also fairly resistant to temperature and humidity changes. It can be worked easily and polished to a high gloss. Layered wood can be had in many colors and color combinations, in which the individual layers are colored differently. It is reasonably priced and is especially valued by the newcomers among the knifemakers.

Because of its stability and insensitivty, layered wood is also used for gun butts and pistol grips. The wooden shafts of Russian hand weapons, for example, are almost all made of layered wood, and the German 98K carbine was also made with layered wood butts during the war. While plastic has meanwhile largely replaced wood in military weapons, competition guns in particular are made with layered wood butts.

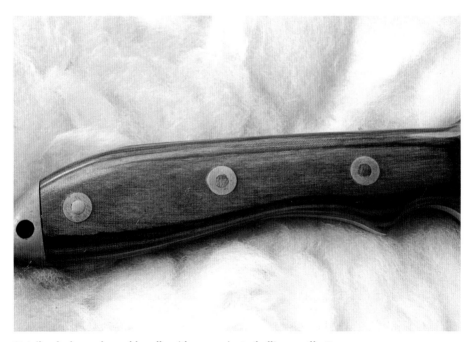

Details of a layered wood handle with screw rivets (bull's-eye effect).

POLISHING WOOD

For the working of wood, the same rules generally apply as with metal. High-quality sandpaper can be used with sanding blocks. Since most knife handles are somewhat rounded, hard rubber makes a good intermediate layer between the wooden block and the sandpaper.

For transitions, though, one must be careful with rubber layers, since the wood, uncontrolled, comes off faster than the metal. Thus slightly messy transitions can result. Therefore it is advisable to work on the transitions from the handle material to the metal with hard sandpaper backing. The combination of hard and soft underlying layers has proved itself. The surface should be sanded as finely as possible, with 600 or 800 grit paper. Only then should the wood be treated with polish. Since wood is often very varied in its structure, with annual rings, branches and growths, wavy surfaces could result from polishing with the soft disc. For this reason it is better to sand problematic wood very finely first and then treat the wood with wood oil, linseed or shellac products (using a soft cloth). These materials close the pores in wood, make it more resistant and bring out the grain better. A fine matte gloss lasts longest, as it retains it looks longer than a high-gloss surface.

Dark sanding dust can work its way into the surface of light wood while it is being worked. If the wood is sealed before the working, this danger is cut down. Wood fillers from modelmaking or a fine sanding base work well. These lacquers dry quickly and allow an uncomplicated overcoating before every change of the sandpaper grade. At the end, more of the grain is brought out by damp sanding with linseed oil, and the wood is then sealed with shellac or tung-oil products.

Shellac is a resinlike substance that is taken from gravid females of the lac bug, *Coccus lacca.* The larvae of the lac bug develop in

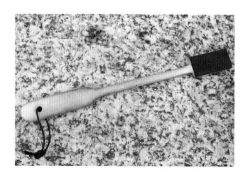

A hard rubber sanding tool.

this layer of resin, In India and Thailand, when phonograph records were still made of shellac, great quantities were produced. For a kilogram of shellac, some 300,000 lac bugs are needed. Shellac is also used to produce lacquer for violin building.

Tung oil is made from tree seeds of the *Euphorbiaceae* family, which grow mainly in China.

Shellac and tung oil are available in the knife-supply trade.

A few preliminary tests on wood of the handle type are often very valuable.

Small cavities turn up again and again in rootwood. Something can be done about this. Smooth the place with fine sandpaper until the hole has filled with sanding dust. Then apply quick-drying glue. After it dries, sand over it and repeat the procedure until the results are satisfactory. A very thick, sandable, and inconspicuous improvement results.

Very oily woods such as thuja, pockwood, or cocobolo quickly clog the sandpaper. With these woods it is advisable to use wet sandpaper along with linseed oil. In this way the sandpaper remains unclogged longer, and the wood is impregnated by the oil.

In a physical and chemical sense, there are many different kinds of wood. Thus it is impossible to give universal advice on sealing. Gaining experience and exchanging ideas with colleagues can help.

Horn, Antler and Bone

There is a basic difference between *horns* and *antlers*.

• In horned animals, like the chamois, mountain sheep, buffalo, and cattle, the head weapons are made of a horn structure. They are mounted like bags over long brow projections and constantly grow from below. Thus the oldest part of a horn is its point. Horns are not shed, and are borne by male and female animals.
• The head weapons of antlered animals are made of bone mounted on brow pro-

jections. With few exceptions—the best-known being the reindeer—only males have antlers; they are used in rutting battles, shed in the autumn and grown anew every year. At first they are covered by a so-called cuticle,* which is later worn away. The later coloring of the antler depends on the tree or wood type on which they are rubbed.

HORN AND ANTLER

Buffalo Horn
Knifemakers usually use the horn of the Indian water buffalo, which has a striking black color. There are also pieces with nice white stripes, which form an interesting contrast to the basic black color. For knife-making, one should use only well-seasoned pieces, as strong shrinking and warping can result otherwise. Buffalo horn should be roughened and degreased before gluing.

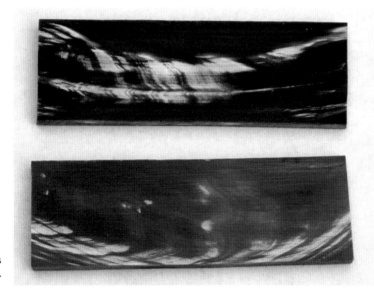

Handle panels of buffalo horn.

---

* Hairy, blooded skin, which surrounds the antler during its formation and supplies it with food and material. After this phase ends, the cuticle dries and is "rubbed off" by the animal on branches, twigs, and young trees.

Kudu Horn

The horn of the greater Kudu, a large antelope living in southern Africa and bearing stately spiral horns, also makes good handle material. It shrinks somewhat less than buffalo horn and has a fine grain.

Light kudu horn.

Dark kudu horn. Knife by Ernst G. Siebeneicher-Hellwig.

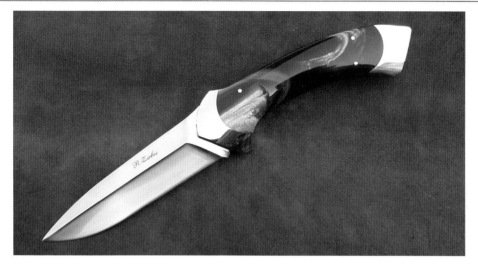

Buffalo horn on a knife by Richard Zirbes.

Sheep Horn

To obtain usable handle material, sheep horn is softened in warm water and then pressed into blocks. Then it must be well seasoned. Sheep horn is slightly transparent, and its surface feels pleasant. Since sheep horn can be transparent in several places, it is advisable to create an optical

Sheep horn.

Sheep horn, knife by Ernst G. Siebeneicher-Hellwig.

division with intermediate layers of fiber. Otherwise the metal handle might shine through under some conditions.

Deer Horn

There are enormous differences here. The best quality for knifemaking comes from the sambar deer of India. Its antlers are scarcely to be had any more, as the Indian authorities have banned its export. This step was necessary to protect the animals form hunters who stalked them for their profitable antlers.

It can generally be seen that antlers from eastern Europe have more bone mass than those of central or western Europe. They have greater wall strength and less spongy core in the middle. Thus antler material from eastern Europe, like that of the famed

Sheep-horn handle panel.

Carpathian deer, is more usable for knifemaking. Naturally, there are also strong, good-quality antlers in central Europe, as deer populations are fed mineral-rich foods, which aids in forming antlers.

Deer horn from the basal area—the thickenings at the base of the antlers—is very useful in knifemaking, since the horn, as already noted, has especially thick walls there. When choosing a piece of antler, one should also note the color and pearling.

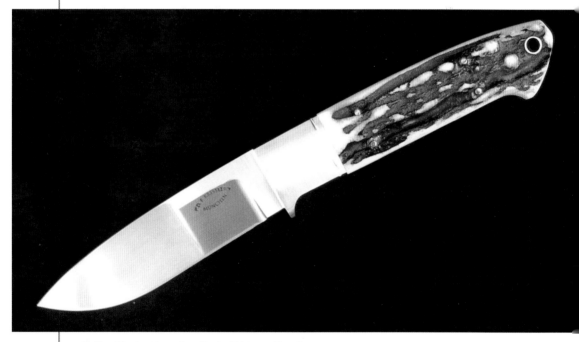

Knife with deer-horn handle, by Dietmar Kressler.

Elk Horn

Here too, the knifemaker values the basal sections particularly. Elk antlers can be used completely for knifemaking. The scoops are suitable for handle panels and the points can be used on curved-tang knives.

Elk horn.

Reindeer Horn

The antlers of the reindeer (called caribou in North America) is, along with birchwood, the most characteristic material for handles of Nordic knives. It is also used to make exquisite scabbards. Reindeer horn can be polished and colored well.

Working tips: As noted, horn should be well seasoned, since it shrinks. Otherwise, unpleasant surprises will turn up. When working it, absolutely wear a *breath mask*. Fine horn dust penetrates into the breathing organs and can do damage. When doing machine work, be sure that the horn does not get hot.

Horn develops unpleasant odors when worked, which demand much understanding from those around you.

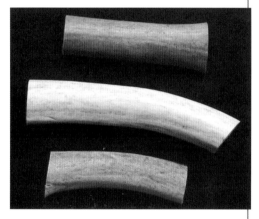

Rolls of reindeer antler

Knife and sheath of reindeer antler; knife by Wolfgang Biegi.

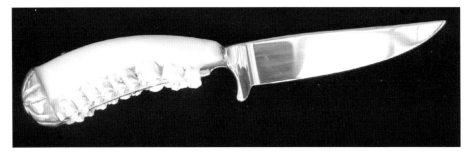

Wild boar jawbone.

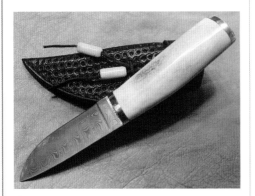

Wapiti horn; knife by Heinrich Schmidbauer.

BONE

Bone has a fine-pored structure, can be colored, and is also suitable for scrimshaw engraving. To get good results, bone must be fat-free (cook it out!) and well seasoned.

Cattle and Camel Bone

Outwardly, they resemble ivory, but are much less expensive and are not legally protected. They are also easy to work. Older bones take on a patina that adds to their charm.

Giraffe bone on a knife by
Andreas Schweikert.

Fossil Bone

The buyer should make sure that the bones have not turned to stone. Otherwise, working with typical tools and methods is not possible. Bones of ancient horses, bison, woolly rhinoceros, deer, and mammoths from the last Ice Age (8000 to 13,000 years ago) are available. Cracks in the material should be filled with polishable plastic (acrylic or quick glue). Fossil bones look good with their usually brownish and well-polished surfaces.

Antler of an ancient deer; knife by Heinrich Schmidbauer.

Handle made from old deer bone that knifemaker Heinrich Schmidbauer found in his hunting range.

Materials

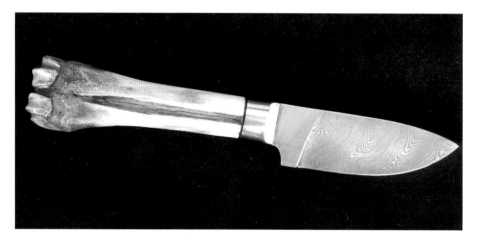

Wild horse bone; knife by Hans Joachim Faust.

Sea-cow bone; knife by Ernst G. Siebeneicher-Hellwig.

Whale jawbone; knife by Gerd Ohnesorge.

Oosic

The penis bone of the walrus is a very exclusive handle material. Oosic has a very fine-pored bone structure. Nicely colored fossil pieces are very popular but very rare.

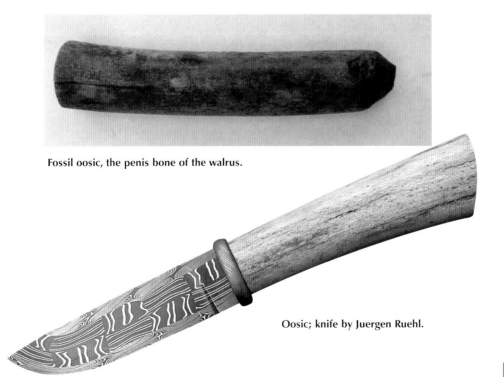

Fossil oosic, the penis bone of the walrus.

Oosic; knife by Juergen Ruehl.

71

Materials

Stabilized and Colored Bone

As with stabilized wood, the fine capillaries of the bone are filled with colored or colorless acrylic resin. Bone then shrinks less and takes on nice color effects, while the typical structure is kept. Primarily giraffe bone, oosic, sea-cow, and cattle bone are treated by this method.

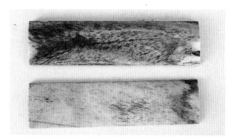

Colored giraffe bone.

For this knife, Ernst G. Siebeneicher-Hellwig chose giraffe-bone handle panels.

Here one sees the broad palette of colored giraffe bone. Knives by Helmut Iffland.

Mother-of-pearl

Horst Heinle

Nature shows her vast variety in mussels and sea snails. The beauty of their patterns, colors, and shapes has inspired man for ages.

Mussels have two shells that are hinged together at their upper rim. They are made mostly of calcium carbonate, built up in thin layers. Mother-of-pearl is the hard, shimmering inner layer that forms in mussel and univalve shells. The fine play of color is formed by breaking entering light rays.

Many knifemakers who use mother-of-pearl for handles to give knives a higher value scarcely think about where this material comes from. And if they did, they would still not have a bad conscience, though certain species have been brought to the verge of extinction because of their shells. This danger does in fact exist, but is not because of mother-of-pearl, which is not the reason for overfishing. Such mussels are caught for their flesh. So it is not a matter of glimmering shells, but their content. The shell is merely a "waste product."

Knife with mother-of-pearl handle panels, by Richard Zirbes.

Knife by Stefan Steigerwald, with mother-of-pearl handle panels.

Probably the most frequently used type of mother-or-pearl is popularly known as *Macassar shell*. Its generic Latin name is *Pinctada*. The nicest mother-of-pearl comes from this creature, which lives in the waters around Australia, the Philippines and the South Pacific.

The largest species of this type, which provides the thick mother-of-pearl shells for knifemaking and jewelry, (its almost round diameter can be 20 cm and more), is called *Pinctada maxima*.

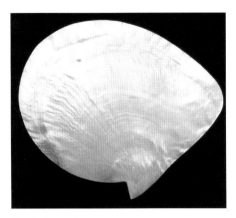

Pinctada maxima

Its inside radiates a tender, silky glow. Unless the outer shell is cleaned completely to "white mother-of-pearl", it has a yellowish sheen. This yellow mother-of-pearl is also called *Gold Lip* and offers the knifemaker a change from "white mother-of-pearl."

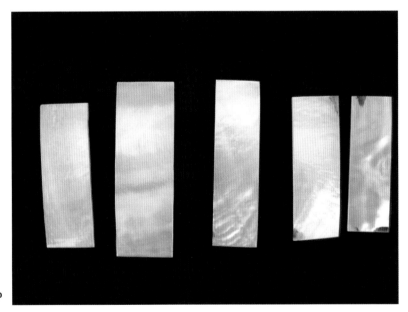

Gold Lip

Abalone Shell *(Haliotis)*
Abalone is actually not a mussel, but a sea snail with only one outer shell. This genus, which also forms mother-of-pearl, includes over 100 species worldwide, especially in the Indian and Pacific oceans, in the Atlantic off western Africa, and in the Mediterranean. Only the larger types—when some 20 cm long they are thought to be about 13 years old—produce usable mother-of-pearl. They are also called *Meerohr (Haliotis mi-*

dae). The inside of the shell is mostly covered with an iridescent mother-of-pearl (shimmering red, green, gold and blue tones).

Mosaic Abalone
Beautiful and sufficiently large pieces of abalone shell are rare and expensive. Mosaic abalone, which consists of abalone pieces poured into artificial resin, can also be used as a really lovely alternative.

Mosaic Abalone.

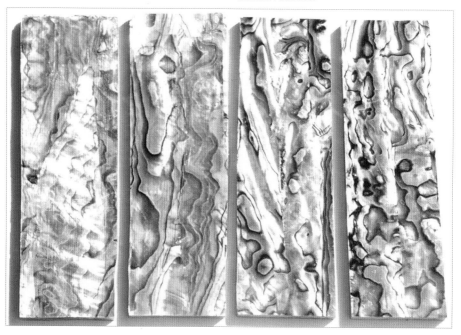

Mosaic abalone; knife by Ernst G. Siebeneicher-Hellwig.

Paua Shell (Haliotis iris)

The Paua is also a sea snail; it lives only in New Zealand's clear, clean, mineral-rich South Pacific coastal waters. The Maori, original inhabitants of New Zealand, gave this unusual creature the name of "Paua." The animal is protected by a quota system, which assures that the species is not threatened with extinction. It is probably the most beautiful and unusual snail in the world.

The valuable and richly colored shells, with their intensive blue and green tones plus hints of pink and other colors, are also of interest to knifemakers. The shell measures about 12 cm, which means that only small plates of about 25 x 46 mm and some 2 mm thick can be made.

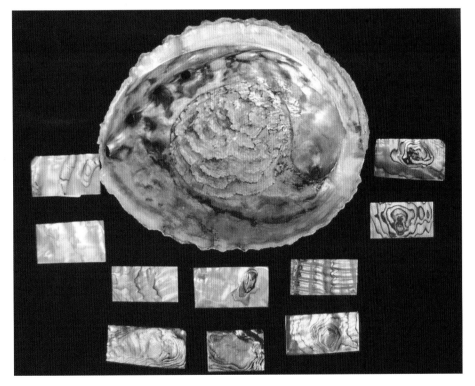

Abalone shell and Paua pieces.

MOTHER-OF-PEARL WORK

Mother-of-pearl does not shrink or change its shape after being made into handle panels. When it is smoothed or shaped, the piece should not be heated excessively, as this can result in deep burn marks that are very hard to remove. Mother-of-pearl can also be worked like bone or ivory. When holes are bored in it, a mineral liquid should be used as a coolant. One or two drops are quite sufficient. When riveting it, a little superglue (quick-drying) should be out into the hole. This will keep polishing paste away from the borehole and also prevent a change of color, since no oil can penetrate at this place. But always remember that mother-of-pearl is translucent. It is only a little harder than bone and can be cut with a jigsaw or goldsmith's saw. Cutting or polishing work should only be done with good ventilation, since the shell smells unpleasant when worked and the dust is not healthful.

Engraving can be done to mother-of-pearl similarly to metal. The graving tool must be sharpened a little more and held a little differently. A few minutes' practice will generally suffice to give the engraver a "feel" for engraving mother-of-pearl. The best examples of old English and European utensils had very nicely engraved and cut mother-of-pearl handles.

Carving of mother-of-pearl is an art of its own. Because of the relative softness and great stability of the material, mother-of-pearl has been used for centuries as a material for creative art.

Scrimshaw techniques (needle engraving filled in with color) generally afford very lovely results. Around the turn of the 20th century, it was the fashion to decorate utensils with needle-engraved mother-of-pearl handles. Today they are treasured as museum pieces. There is scarcely any scrimshaw engraving done with mother-of-pearl now, since it is harder than ivory.

Ivory

Horst Heinle

Ivory refers primarily to the material gained from the tusks of the elephant and its ancestors. Among the elephant's ancestors were the *Mastodon,* which lived about 100,000 years ago, and the *Mammoth,* which may have died out only 5000 years ago. In addition, a number of valuable materials are called ivory that resemble it in appearance and structure. For the knifemaker, chiefly elephant ivory (the still-living type), mammoth ivory, walrus tusks, hippopotamus teeth, narwhal teeth, and wart-hog teeth are available.

Characteristics of Ivory

Ivory is a tooth substance and not a bone material like many ivory substitutes (bone or deer antler). It differs from bone primarily through its low mineral content. This explains its greater elasticity in particular, but also its greater resistance to breakage and ability to be polished, as well as the minimal brittleness of the thickly structured ivory compared to the porous bone material. In fresh condition, ivory has a water content of 25%, which sinks to about 15% after air-drying.

The solid components are about 60% tooth bone and 40% cartilage. Tooth bone consists mainly of fluorapatite, a calcium phosphate that contains fluorine. The cartilage consists for the most part of the organic substance dentin, a nitrogen-holding frame albumen material with minerals included, forming a tough elastic mass. The characteristic qualities of ivory, treasured by handcrafters, result from the cooperation of these organic and inorganic substances.

The inner structure of ivory can be recognized by the typical grain. Lengthwise, a network structure reminiscent of wood-grain or formed of diamond-shaped basic elements, can be seen. In cross-section, a rosette pattern that consists of many intersecting ellipses appears. These structural elements allow real ivory to be easily distinguished from all its imitators.

Because of its comparatively high content of dentin and other organic substances, ivory is hygroscopic (attracting water) and thus fairly sensitive to overheating, cooling, and too-high moisture. When cooled for a long time, shrinking of the collage (cartilage) occurs, which leads to loss of elasticity and—under mechanical pressure—to cracking, as can be seen in mammoth ivory. When overheated, perhaps by radiant warmth or in pieces that get into the vicinity of the soldering flame, cracks are caused by drying. Singed surfaces cannot be cleaned by bleaching, and must be removed by grinding or similar means.

Elephant Ivory

This is obtained from the more or less curved tusks of African or Asiatic ("Indian") elephants. At their lower ends, the tusks are hollow (1/2 to 2/3 of the overall length). The massive tip has a "nucleus" that consists of nerve fibers and is an identifying mark of real ivory. The cross-section of the tusks is oval, but comes close to being circular. Size and color differ according to origin. The tusks of African elephants reach an average length of 2 to 3 meters, a diameter of 15-16 cm at their thickest point, and a weight of 45 to 80 kg. Their color varies among yellowish, greenish or reddish tones (in West African ivory types). West African ivory is faintly transparent (called "glassbone" in the trade). East African ivory, though, is opaque and a dull milky white (called "milkbone" in the trade). All African ivory types can be polished well, are strongly structured and relatively hard.

A Bowie knife with ebony handle panels and ivory carving; knife by Helmut Iffland.

Tusks of Asiatic (mostly Indian) elephants are smaller (1 to 1.5 meters) and weigh 20 to 30 kg. Their ivory is snow-white at first (only ivory from Thailand is reddish), but yellows rather quickly. The African types prevail on the European ivory market. Asiatic ivory, though, is hard to come by. We are talking here, of course, only of legally obtained ivory, which has a required certificate and was imported and traded by, or corresponds to, the applicable legal requirements.

Mammoth Ivory

This fossil ivory comes from the strongly curved tusks, up to 5 meters long, of the extinct mammoth. It has been found in caves in southern France, the Urals of Russia, and especially in Siberian ice. A millennia-long hardening process has made it harder and heavier than other types of ivory. Its quality suffers from countless small hairline cracks and it is comparatively cheap.

Pieces colored turquoise blue by injection of vivianite (an iron phosphate) are found in the trade as so-called *tooth turquoise* or *odontoliths*. Siberian mammoth ivory was once imported into central Europe by the Vikings, the master weaponmakers and traders who began to trade with the Orient. Today it is scarcely to be found in Germany.

Horst Heinle

For the possession and trade of ivory and other legally protected natural materials, there are detailed legal regulations. In case of doubt, it is best to inquire about the exact regulations at the appropriate government offices, so as to avoid legal conflicts.

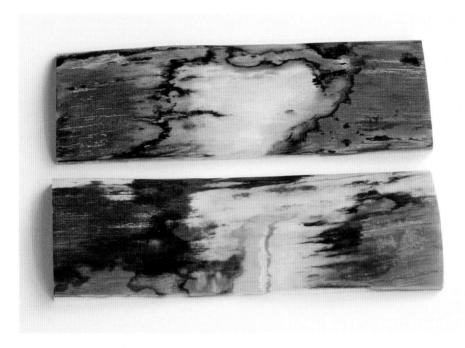

Mammoth tusk, panels with different-colored outer skin.

A piece of mammoth tusk.

Mammoth tusk, knife by Richard Spizl.

Materials

Mammoth tusk panels with reddish-brown outer skin.

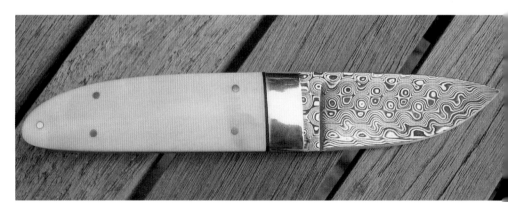

Mammoth-ivory handle from the tusk's core; knife by Hubert Ziegler.

Walrus Tusks

Walrus tusks are more like ivory than any other material in use. They are 40 to 75 cm long and weigh 2 to 3 kg (at most, 1 meter long and some 3.5 kg). A kind of marbling can be found inside them, surrounded by hard enamel. This feature can serve to identify them, since it occurs only in walrus tusks.

Walrus-tusk; knife by Gerd Ohnesorge.

Hippopotamus Teeth

The hippopotamus provides a very hard, white, only slightly yellowing type of ivory. It comes from the animal's eight incisors and four canine teeth. The two canines of the lower jaw, that are curved in half-moon shape and sharply angled at the points, yield especially good ivory. These teeth are 40 to 60 cm long and weigh 4 to 5 kg. Hippo ivory is the hardest ivory. The outer layer of dentin is especially resistant.

Hippopotamus tooth and ibex horn, with a fountain pen for size comparison.

Narwhal Teeth

This is by far the most expensive quality of ivory, and was worth its weight in gold for centuries. It is the hollow left tusk of the narwhal *(Monodon monoceros)*, up to three meters long and forming a clockwise spiral. The right tusk is usually vestigial. The animal once owed its name of *Unicorn* or *Einhorn* to this condition. From ignorance of the origin of the tooth, it was thought to come from a fabled beast resembling a horse. Since the unicorn's horn enjoyed the reputation of an excellent antidote to poison in the Middle Ages, the teeth were very often worked into cups that were supposed to protect their owners from poisoned drinks.

Narwhal teeth are harder and more brittle that ivory. Their color is pure white, their structure extraordinarily fine. They differ from other ivory-type materials in having faint concentric circles that are recognizable in the cross-section.

Narwhal tooth; knife by Stefan Steigerwald.

Wart-hog Teeth

The tusks of the wart-hog make ideal handle material for curved-tang knives, since their size and shape make them fit well into the hand.

The knifemaker scarcely needs to work the tooth. Thus wart-hog teeth are also suitable handle material for the beginner. It can also be cut and worked as handle panels for pocket knives and full-tang knives.

Wart-hog teeth can be had in the trade. The prices vary, although the material is inherently fine, but are still in reasonable bounds.

Horst Heindle

Wart-hog tusks.

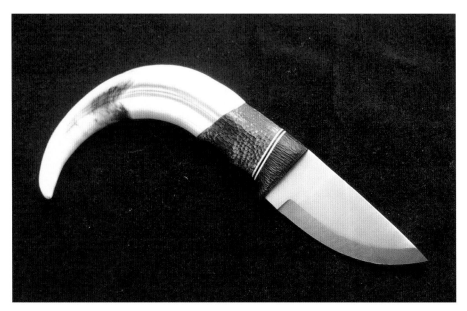

Wart-hog tusk; knife by Holger Fieck.

Wart-hog tusk; knife by Manfred Ritzer.

Other Handle Materials

Fiber-reinforced Plastics

Fiber-reinforced plastics are absolutely "high-tech" materials. They come originally from the aerospace industry and passed via auto racing (Formula 1) to auto building in general, and to knifemaking.

The advantages are obvious: Low weight, relatively high firmness, stability, and corrosion resistance. They can be worked easily and do not feel really cold even in cold weather. In their manufacture, plaited mats of fibrous material are laid over each other and poured into plastic. The material hardens under pressure and heat.

The market offers carbon-fiber plastics for knife handles. They are used especially often for knives that are to be as light as possible, such as those for long-distance hikers (trekking), mountain climbers, and expedition members. But more and more collectors are also discovering that they like knives with plastic handles, especially for their interesting optics.

In making handles of carbon-fiber materials, the worker absolutely must use breathing protection. The dust is highly dangerous for the bronchia.

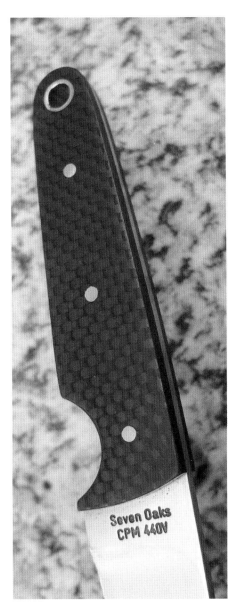

A handle made of carbon-fiber material.

Semiprecious Stones

Minerals are also used gladly for handles because of their optical qualities. Because of their hardness, many semiprecious stones cannot be worked with normal tools. Tools from the jewelry (diamond) industry are needed here.

Another disadvantage of minerals is their tendency to break—what is hard, breaks easily. Gemstones are thus one of the decorative elements for knives, for example, in the form of inlays.

Naturally, an advantage of gemstones is their rigidity. One does not need to worry about shrinkage in their case.

There are also semiprecious stones that can be worked with ordinary tools. The relatively soft lapis lazuli can even be filed, though somewhat laboriously. This stone has the Mohs hardness of 5.

By the way, the Mohs scale of hardness indicates the hardness of rocks and minerals. The scale has ten units, with diamond being

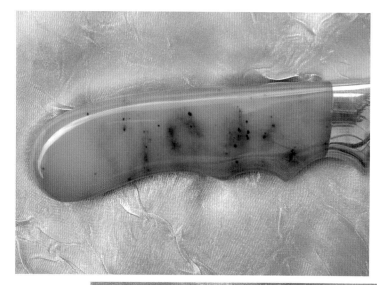

Knife handle panels of jade; knife by Juergen Christmann.

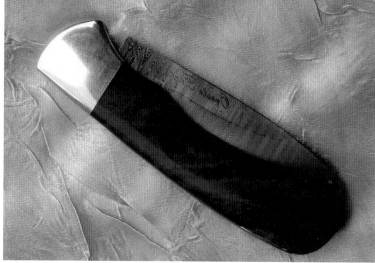

Knife handle panels of lapis lazuli; knife by Juergen Christmann.

number 10. Talc, for example, is number 1, as is the enamel of mammoth teeth. One can scrape material off them with a fingernail.

As a rule of thumb, if the material can be scratched with a fingernail, it has Mohs hardness 2.5. Materials of hardness 3 can be scratched with a copper coin. Those with hardness 5 can be scratched with a knife. Materials with greater hardness can be worked only with hard metals or diamonds.

Here are the hardnesses of some knife-handle materials:

Tiger-eye	7	Malachite	4
Jade	7	Amber	2.5
Garnet	7.5	Coral	3.5
Pyrite	6	Mother-	
Corundum	9	of-pearl	3.5
Turquoise	5.5		

Handle panels of petrified wood; knife by Ernst G. Siebeneicher-Hellwig.

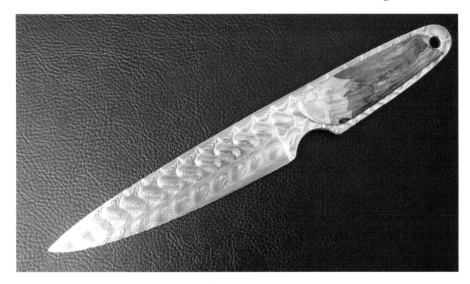

Handle panels of tiger-eye; knife by Juergen Christmann.

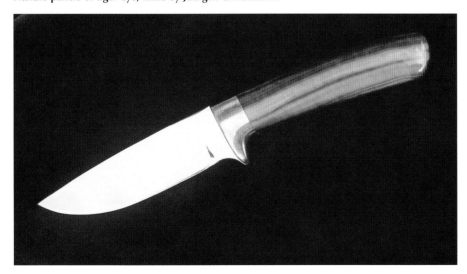

Artificial Semiprecious Stones

The trade offers a wide variety of synthetic jewels. Whoever wants to can obtain turquoise, malachite, agate, onyx, lapis lazuli, coral and many other such stones. The material is offered in plates, which much simplifies its use. It is very easy to work, and the stones can be brought to a high gloss with the usual polishing procedures and materials. The synthetic creations offer the beauty of the natural gems at far more reasonable prices, with the added advantage of being workable with ordinary tools.

The synthetic stones are made of dust and broken pieces of real gems, which are left over in the jewelry industry. The dust is mixed with acrylic resin and pressed into plates. For the classy knife fan, of course, the genuine gem is more interesting.

Malachite inlays in an integral knife made by Gernot Loquai.

A knife with mammoth ivory and an inlay of artificial lapis lazuli.

Micarta®

Micarta® is a synthetic handle material. It is made by soaking paper, linen, or rags in phenol resin and then hardening it.

Micarta® is easy to work and remains stable, not warping or shrinking. Micarta® can be polished well and makes a good optical impression. It feels pleasant, even when cold, and is very economical. Micarta can be had as plates, blocks, and angles, in various colors. Ivory-colored Micarta is popular, since it looks very much like natural bone or ivory. The American veteran knifemaker Bob Loveless has found this material to be popular with knife fans.

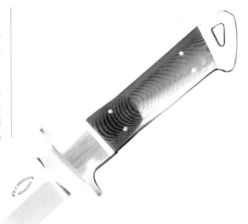

Linen Micarta; knife by Dietmar Kressler.

Below: Tanto by Erich Hanneder, with ray skin and silk wrapping.

Tanto Wrapping

The *Tanto,* the traditional dagger of the Japanese Samurai, was—like the sword—usually fitted with a handle that was underlain with ray skin and wrapped with silken cords.

Making such a traditional handle is very laborious and requires some practice. But the result charms through its fine-looking handle that lies comfortably in the hand. This type of handle formation is less suited for practical use, since it is sensitive to dirt.

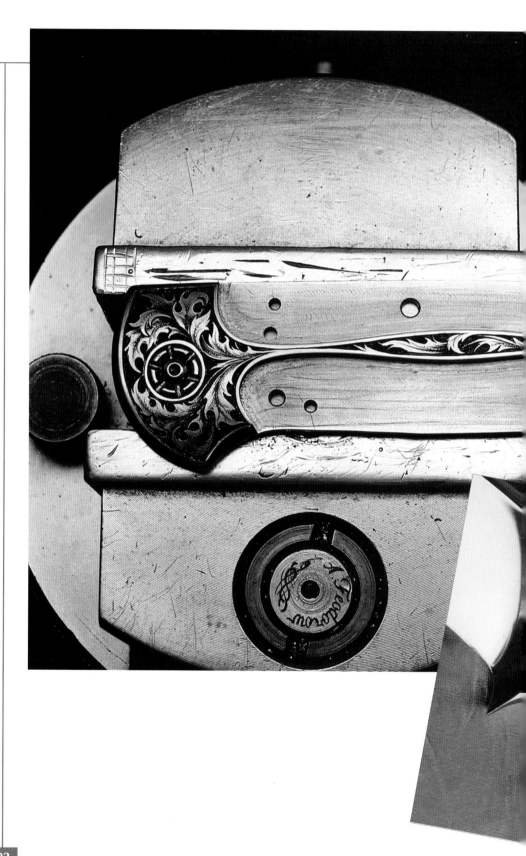

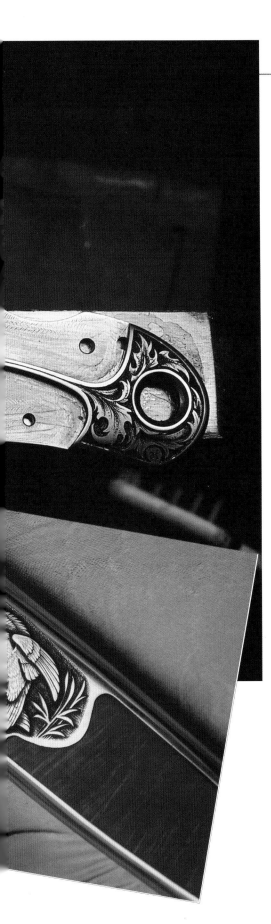

Decorative Techniques

Engraving

Richard "Ritchi" Maier

Engraving ranks among the oldest art forms of mankind. Its development is a long, interesting story. What is important here concerns engraving and knives, for these two themes have gone the same paths as long as they have existed.

It has always been part of human nature to decorate things with which man surrounded himself, to ornament them and thus make them into individual objects—as individual as the man himself.

Anyone who has had a handmade knife produced to suit his own wishes is seeking something out of the ordinary. The conceptions of the client as to material and shape are turned into such a knife. To complete this individuality, it is appropriate to ennoble the knife with the styling element of engraving.

But this ennobling becomes ever harder. Hand engravers are threatened with "extinction." Fewer and fewer young people learn an artistic handicraft in these days of "high tech" and computers. One does not easily find these artists in the telephone book.

Thus the first step is the search for a suitable engraver. Specialist magazines and the Internet are often helpful here. Another way to make contact is to visit an appropriate fair or exhibition. There one also picks up impressions of the quality and style of the engraving work, and one often meets the corresponding engraver in person. Thus one can make clear in a preliminary talk whether the conceptions fit together and will result in collaboration.

Here too, the right advice is very important. The client's wishes, the work, and the price must be brought to a common denominator with the aspects of the knife. For example, there would be little sense to having 5000 Euro worth of engraving applied to a 1500-Euro knife.

Style elements and materials of the knife should also be considered in choosing the design and engraving technique. The engraving should blend into a unity with the knife. For therein is the secret of a beautiful engraving that ennobles the knife.

Engraving Techniques

For knifemaking, the following techniques usually come into consideration.

- Bullino engraving, chasing, or plastic (relief) engraving,
- Flat engraving

BULLINO ENGRAVING

BASICS:
Bullino engraving is most comparable with the technique of steel engraving or, for example, with cold-needle etching. Depressions and lines are created on the worked surface through manual pressure on the various engraving tools. The resulting engraved lines create various shadow effects that the engraver makes use of for his motif.

With the use of fine needles, the engraver's conceptions can be realized more spontaneously than, for example, with metal engraving.

The origin of bullino engraving is attributable to the Italian school of engraving. Italian engravers named it after the tool often used for it, the "bullino graver."

REALMS OF USE:
Traditionally, the technique of bullino engraving is related to the ornamentation of fine rifles and hunting guns. It is found more and more, though, in the engraving of high-priced knives. The aspect of jewelry engraving should not be forgotten.

On knives it is, above all, the guard elements, material inlays on the handle, screws and rivets, or more rarely, the blade area, that are decorated with the bullino technique.

THE MOST IMPORTANT TOOLS:
Engraving needle (diamond-shaped head), steel needle, pointed needle (pointed oval, cap), loupes, microscope, pencils, coloring materials (black lacquer and paint), white undercoat, hand whetstone, steel ruler, cleaning cloth.

SUITABLE ENGRAVING MEDIA:
Various steels and steel alloys (considering the possible surface hardening of the engraved object), precious metals (such as gold and silver alloys), bright metals (such as German silver, copper, brass), titanium, aluminum.

THE MOST IMPORTANT TECHNIQUES:
Point, line and mixing techniques.

Left: Bullino engraving by "Ritchi" Maier.

Opposite: Flat engraving by Kati Mau on a knife by Richard Zirbes.

MOTIFS:
The choice of motifs and their application belongs in the end to the engraver and the client themselves. The ability to apply the chosen motif is important. Here viewpoints like size relations, composition, placing, and, not least, the type of motif are to be considered. In an ideal case, the theme of the engraving should always correspond with the theme of the knife. An example:

For an Alpine-style hunting knife with a deer-horn handle, the subjects of red deer, black deer, oak leaves, etc., are natural. An elephant or Indian head would be out of place here.

WORK PROCESSES:
An appropriate chosen or designed motif is applied to the surface in question. For this, the finely smoothed and well-polished surface is covered with white undercoat.

On this matte white surface, the engraver now draws the motif. Appropriate high points and uneven areas in the engraving surface (distortions of perspective) must be noted. The drawing, which required a certain artistic talent, is best done with fine pencils (0.3-mm leads).

In the next step, the appropriate contours and important lines of the motif are made with fine steel needles and the white paint is removed.

Now the real engraving process begins under the loupe, or depending on the degree of fineness, the microscope. The engraver begins to cut the appropriate lines into the surface. The motif and the artistic interpretation determine the type of the chosen linees. For example, it makes sense to portray the fur structure of a bear with variously long lines rather than points. "The last word" here naturally is that of the engraver.

To make the engraving more "visible," coloring is done with various media (lacquers and oxidizing means). Here there is no single patented recipe. It depends on the factors of material, engraving technique, depth, and motif.

The white undercoat is removed with the finest smoothing and polishing means. This requires some fingertip feeling and practice, for too much removal can lighten the engraving too much and can make it look "un-sharp".

Finally, if advisable, certain parts of the motif can be brightened up with various steel polishers and whetting needles.

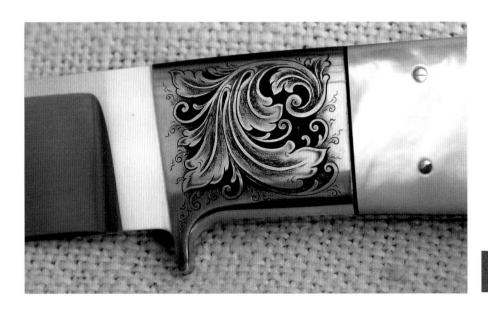

FLAT ENGRAVING

Flat engraving is probably the most often-used engraving technique for lettering, ornaments and motifs of all kinds. The tools used are digging, pointed, ball, line and flat needles, which differ in their cuts. Thus by using various needles one can create various light and dark values. Various punches can also be used, either for the surficial background or in plastic engraving, for the chasing and smoothing of the metal.

Above all, there is the design, which can be created to the client's wishes as bullino, steel, or flat engraving with a deepened background.

The contours are then drawn on the steel to be worked and fixed with a ripping needle, so that they cannot get rubbed off during the engraving.

Depending on the technique used, these lines are either cut with hammer and chisel or by hand with the engraving needle. The next step is the preparation of the background. One can either deepen the background and then punch it to bring out the motif better, or engrave a landscape, depending on the motif.

The next step is shadowing the motif. For this one uses a specially ground needle. By the arrangement of the cuts, as plastic an effect as possible is created. With the narrow cut of the shadowing needle, only a little light can fall into the cut, creating contrasting light and dark values. Finally, the engraving has to be finished, but of that, more later...

A deep flat engraving on a knife by M. Jankowsky

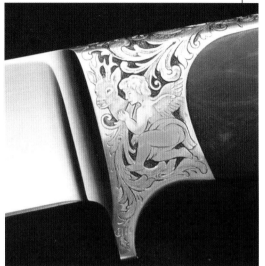

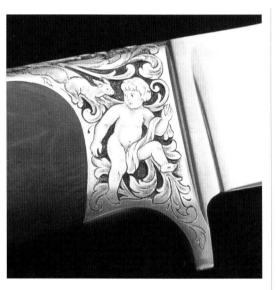

Flat engraving details on Jankowsky's knife.

Flat engraving: the outlines are cut.

Flat engraving: a further step of the work.

Flat engraving: a further step of the work.

Finished flat engraving by engraver Alexandra Feodorow.

CHASING OR PLASTIC ENGRAVING (RELIEF ENGRAVING)

Alexandra Feodorow

In chasing, the chosen motif is cut three-dimensionally with flat and ball chisels. Then it is chased with various round and flat punches and smoothed at the same time.

To increase the plastic effect, the background is deepened and worked with pearl or matte punches. Fine details are made with the digging or pointed needle. To increase the plastic effect, another shadowing is added, with which one can redefine various structures such as fur or scales.

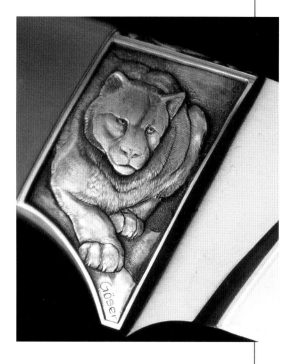

Relief engraving by Goeser on a knife by Richard Zirbes.

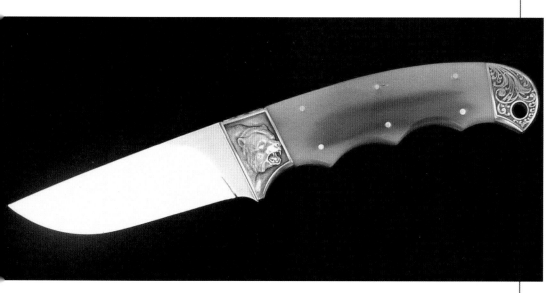

A full view of the knife, taken from the other side.

Decorative Techniques

Relief engraving by Edgar Apel, after an old Japanese woodcut, on a knife by Herbert Schirmer.

Depending on what metal is being engraved, the final treatment must be carried out in order to protect the engraving from corrosion. Most steels can be hardened, whereby the engraving is best protected, since hardened steel does not rust as readily. Many steels can also be hardened colorfully, whereby gold and silver inlays come out especially beautifully. Finally, the engraving is treated with printer's blackening, which strengthens the contrasts.

Alexandra Feodorow

Relief engraving by Alexandra Feodorow.

Relief engraving by Alexandra Feodorow.

Etching and Inlaying

ETCHING

By etching metal surfaces, desired optical effects can be created. Usually the etching is done by the so-called *masking technique*. Asphalt lacquer, such as copperplate engravers use, is good for this. The motif to be etched remains free; the rest is covered with the lacquer. One can also cover the entire surface with the lacquer and cut the motif into the lacquer. For this, though, asphalt lacquer is somewhat too smeary. A harder lacquer is more suitable. Try it with nail polish; red undercoat (from the cosmetic trade), or tracing paint (from the tool trade) should go first.

The suitable acids also depend on the metal to be etched. For rust-free steels, an etching rod used to sign works sometimes does the job. The acid in the rod attacks almost everything but is very "friendly" to the undercoats.

With the help of etching techniques, false Damascus blades can also be made. So beware of low-priced Damascus knives!

False (etched) rose Damascus.

Many artists also go to the trouble of laying out their motifs on translucent foil. They light a photosensitive lacquer undercoat with UV light and apply it to the metal. After lighting, the lacquer is developed in etching natron, exposing the places that are to be etched. Then they can be etched. This process is used mainly in the production of leader plates.

For etching, tests can determine how the acid reacts with the lacquer and how clearly the pattern comes out.

For cases in which patterns or drawings are repeated, such as in signing blades, the electrochemical process is well suited. Here an electrode and an electrolyte bath are used to remove small particles from the

Detailed view of the false Damascus.

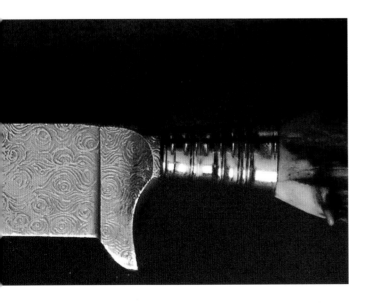

metal. Masking is done with a thin foil that the electrolyte can pass through at the desired places (for example, the writing). For this work, one must obtain a foil and have direct and alternating current. The specialist trade offers such equipment, and one can also have the foil made.rissen.

A saber with an etched blade, lent by Wolfgang Schlag.

INLAYING

Many signatures, decorative lines and ornamentations would only look good if they were set off from the background in color. One would need to inlay a different-colored metal such as gold or silver.

Our ancestors thought of that too, and decorated swords, belt buckles and horse harness with inlays. There are many splendid discoveries from graves of Germanic warriors of the tribal migration era that the visitor to German museums can admire. The inlaid swords and axes of the Vikings are also famous. Inlaying with gold or silver wire is also known from many other cultures, such as India. There the artists of earlier cultures decorated containers and jewelry by means of inlaying. The process is very old.

The trick in inlaying is that the lines are cut into the basic metal with a special tool.

Unlike ordinary engraving, where the engraver cuts V-shaped lines, the cuts for inlaying are cut back. This means that the cuts, seen in cross-section, are wider at the bottom than at the surface of the metal. It looks like an open V turned upside down. or like a dovetail groove or cut. Now a soft metal wire is driven into the cut and takes on a wedge form. Then the surface is smoothed neatly.

Inlaying work can be included in "normal" engraving: tendril patterns with golden ornamental lines or animal figures in precious metal, surrounded by arabesques. The possibilities are almost unlimited. What can be done technically and its financial aspects can be discussed with the engraver. For this high-priced filigree art, though, the client must expect a waiting period, since he is often not the only one who wants an object decorated by this noble technique.

Inlay by Ruth Wichmann.

Inlay by Alexandra Feodorow.

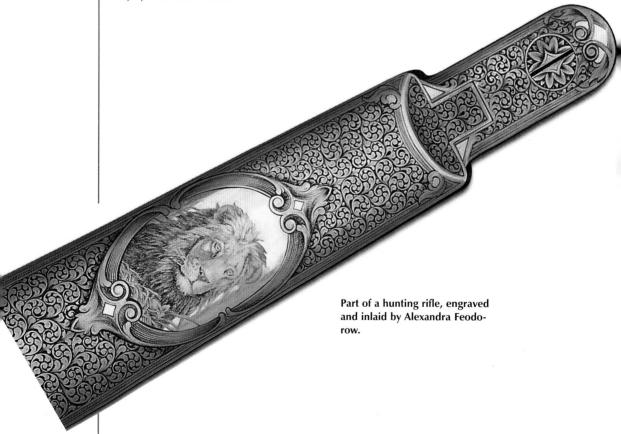

Part of a hunting rifle, engraved and inlaid by Alexandra Feodorow.

Scrimshaw

Eva Halat

Knife handles are also decorated with so-called *Scrimshaw*—colored decorative patterns cut into bone, horn, or ivory. This art has gained greater popularity in Germany and Europe, in fact, in the whole world, in the last 20 to 30 years. Scrimshaw was known chiefly in maritime circles, since its roots are found in this realm. The exact origin of this English word is not known, and it may come from the slang terms of *scrimshin* (a little piece, hunger portion) or *scrimp* (to economize), which were applied to a practice performed on whaling ships where the unusable remains of whales were distributed among the crew.

The Origin of Scrimshaw

If we look very far back in human history, we find, among all the world's peoples, utensils and ritual objects made of horn, bone, or ivory decorated with archaic patterns and symbols. Though not comparable with present-day scrimshaw, the use of these materials and the desire to ornament them is still in our blood. The material has a spirit, as opposed to lifeless plastic. This value is visibly recognized by adding filigreed artwork.

The actual origin of scrimshaw, though, is found among the whalers of the 18th and

Traditional inscribed decorations on a Nordic knife.

Decorative Techniques

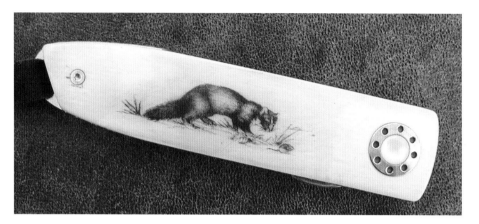

Above: Scrimshaw by Alexandra Feodorow on a knife by Franz Hutzler.

19th centuries. Even before this time there were objects made of whalebone and baleen, a hornlike material from the mouths of baleen whales, that were decorated with this technique. But only with the discovery of the sperm whale and the resulting long voyages of the whaling ships did the real era of scrimshaw begin.

Before then, whalers had caught whales near the coasts, but these were all whales that had no teeth. The catch was brought into the harbor and processed there. Only when a whaler was driven far from the shore in a storm was the sperm whale discovered; it lived farther out in the open sea and had teeth that were especially suitable as the material for the scrimshaw technique.

A faun seizing a nymph. Scrimshaw by Attila Harmat.

Now a different strategy was required to process the whales, for the trip home from the hunting areas took too long. So they began to build larger ships, dissect whales on board, and cook out the blubber. The oil was the real reason for whaling. It was used for lamps, among other things (hence the concept of the whale-oil lamp).

Now a bigger crew was needed for such a ship, more men than were needed for the actual maneuvering of the ship. In whaling, the seamen were responsible for the ship and the whalers for the whales.

When the whaling was done, the oil stowed in barrels and no more whales in sight, a period of idleness began for the whaling crew. During the voyages, which lasted up to five years, the men thought of home, family, or the last dangerous catch of a whale.

There were surely enough usable remains of the whales lying around on the ship, and the teeth of the sperm whale were ideally suited for scrimshaw. So they passed the time by carving motifs whose contents were generally scenes of whaling, sailing ships, girls back home, etc. Various objects, such as corset bones, combs, utensils and other mementos for the dear ones at home were carved out of whalebone and decorated.

With the discovery of petroleum, which provided more valuable oil than whale blubber, whaling quickly came to an end. For a long time, scrimshaw seemed to have been condemned to death, but it was rediscovered in the 1950s. U.S. President Kennedy was one of the best-known collectors of old whale teeth with scrimshaw decoration.

Modern scrimshaw in stippling technique by Kati Mau on a knife by Richard Zirbes.

In the 1980s, big scrimshaw studios, at which the technique was refined to its highest quality, appeared on the east and west coasts of North America. Colorful works and new motifs that had nothing to do with seafaring or whaling were also "scrimmed."

With the passage of the protection law in 1997, the art of scrimshaw seemed to have come to an abrupt end again. The ivory trade was banned or very strongly limited. Nevertheless, scrimshaw has hung on to the present, and has perhaps increased in quality and value as the material becomes more and more costly.

To be sure, the strict laws concerning the buying and selling of various materials that can be "scrimmed" has to be kept in mind. These laws are different in every country, and it is advisable that one check with A responsible authority.

Scrimshaw Materials and Tools

All "scrimmable" materials are suitable for knife handles. But not all handle materials can be decorated with this technique. Wood and linen micarta, for example, are too crude; only paper micarta can be used as a basis for scrimshaw. All horn and ivory, bone (unless petrified), and many plastics and other materials that are thick enough and can be polished smooth enough to carve on them, can be used.

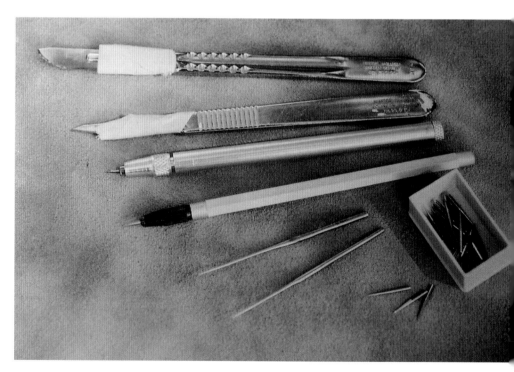

Scrimshaw tools.

There are different hardnesses of ivory. Elephant ivory, and very specifically walrus and mammoth ivory, are outstanding and pleasantly "soft" materials. On the other hand, hippopotamus teeth are, because of their hardness, a real challenge for a scrimshaw artist.

Horn is very soft, but unlike ivory, it consists of very fine fibers that can easily send the engraving needle in the wrong direction. Black buffalo horn is very good for white scrimshaw on a black background.

Bone is the best material, but is somewhat brittle. Beginners are often advised to practice on bone because this material is cheap and easy to obtain. But one really needs some experience to make really good scrimshaw on brittle bone.

Eva Halat at work under the loupe.

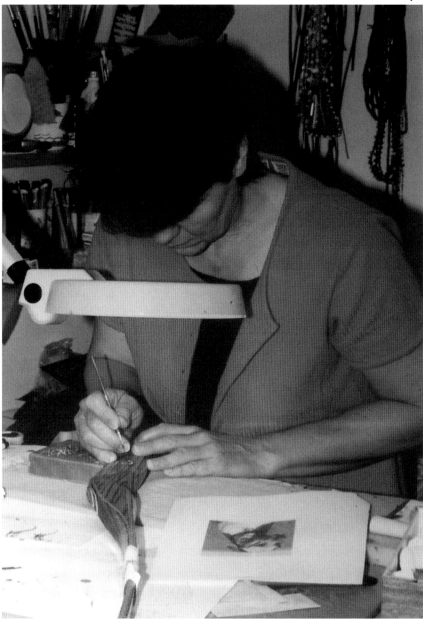

The scrimshaw tool is really just a needle, plus a good loupe or microscope to help out. There are no special scrimshaw tools in the trade. Many artists make their own needles out of old, round mechanic's files, ripping needles, or other pointed objects made of hard steel or other hard metal, which they fit into a suitable holder that fits into the hand well. It is important that the needle has a thin tapering cone, so that the points and lines can be cut very finely and do not become too thick.

For basic equipment, I would recommend a good standing loupe with a light that shines downward. Twofold magnification is completely sufficient. There are also head loupes of varying quality, and, for very fine work, stereo microscopes are also used. Many dealers offer the chance to try out various loupes. One should very definitely use this opportunity, since long work under bad optics is simply impossible.

Colors

Scrimshaw is done with various types of coloring. Water-resistant water and oil paints are classic media, but printer's ink and airbrush paint have been put to use. Many artists also make up their own recipes, which naturally are not made public. Water-resistant watercolor paint dries very quickly on the surface, and must be removed after coloring with water, or, better, with saliva. Oil paint can be removed easily with a cloth or a paper napkin, but takes a long time to dry completely. But splendid results can be attained with either paint.

When buying coloring material for scrimshaw decoration, one must make sure that they are artists' paints of the highest quality, finely and thickly pigmented. These paints are expensive, of course, but with the small quantities needed for scrimshaw work, they last forever.

Working Techniques

The following points that are summed up here should be kept in mind when "scrimming." The surface of the object must be sanded and polished mirror-smooth, so one can work neatly on it. After polishing, the motif is transferred to the surface and cut or punched into the material with the needle in the artist's style or the nature of the motif. To make the motif visible, the color is now rubbed in with a cloth so that the whole "scrimmed" surface is colored. When the superfluous color is wiped off, color is held in the cut or punched depressions and the motif becomes visible. Now it is also clear why no color can remain on the rest of the surface. To be sure that this does not happen, a test coloring of the prepared polished surface is an important step. If the color can be wiped completely off the surface, the work can begin. If a bit of color remains as a gray haze, one must polish the surface again, or even grind it, to remove scratches.

When you have the piece of material with the well-prepared surface lying in front of you, first transfer the motif to the smooth surface. Practiced sketchers can draw it directly onto the material. It is best to use a soft pencil or a special pencil for glass that shows up well on smooth material, but with a somewhat heavier line. This pre-drawing is now reproduced with the needle in very fine points or short lines, only as much as is necessary to retain the most important contours of the motif. After that, the first color is applied.

A different method of putting the motif on the surface is punching. The motif is first brought to the correct size by hand or with a copier or computer. Then it is attached with tape precisely at the place where the finished motif is to be. Now take a needle and punch the contours and important lines

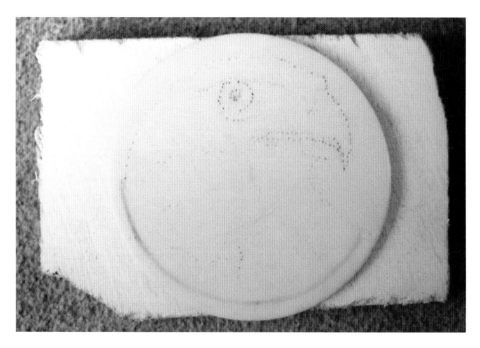

The first points of an eagle's head are made.

that are to be used through the paper and into the surface, and then rub color into the resulting depressions. It tales a bit of fingertip feeling to make the points punched through the paper neither too big nor too small. Too-thick points at the angles of the motif can be disturbing. It is not so bad if the points are so small that one still cannot see them after rubbing in the color. One must simply repeat the whole punching procedure. For this reason it is important to fix the paper with the motif pattern to the surface so that it can be folded to the side to apply the color. To repeat the punching, it has to be returned and fixed exactly in the same position.

The transferred contour points can be completed now with the first gentle lines, small dashes or additional points, so that one

achieves a similar result to the "free" technique of drawing.

Now the actual "scrimming," the working out of the motif, can begin. There are various techniques by which different designs can be portrayed. Every artist chooses a technique that he wants and also develops an individual style. Some punch everything, some use only the very traditional line technique, and others combine the two. When one looks at the work of well-known scrimshaw artists, under strong magnification, one sometimes sees lines in a style that could be called more like drawing.

I am of the opinion that it does not depend on the style. It should, though, be in harmony with one's own feeling, and the technique should harmonize with the motif. Uneven lines and dashes, that look uncertain, as if the artist did not know just why he had made them in this manner, look dilettantish and disturbing. Lines that run counter to the motif, such as falsely structured hair, also look very bad.

With time, with some practice, and with critical observation of the work of other artists, a beginner in this art form can find the way he works best.

The following sketches of the possible portrayals of various surfaces should be encouraging and lead to better understanding of the process. They will help the eginner with experience in drawing and painting tol have considerably less difficulty in finishing an initial good scrimshaw successfully.

The material should be worked with fine lines, which means not cutting too deep, so that the work does not become too crude. The finer, the better. But what must be remembered is that in utilitarian scrimshaw one must work a little deeper, so that the color does not wear off in time. If a work gets hard use, like a pendant that is worn on the skin (sweat is very aggressive), or a knife that is used often, then one should consider whether the work should be coated thinly with a quick-drying lacquer.

It is best to apply the entire motif in what I call the first go-round, and do the first coloring only after that. One works at it so that the surface to be decorated reflects while being worked. Either one holds the piece so that it reflects, or one places the light accor-

Gentle lines arise.

The finished eagle's head.

dingly. The worked places are visible on the reflecting surface without color, since they appear matte as opposed to the gleaming surface.

I do not like to color individual parts of the motif during the first process, because then I have no more comparison of how the worked but not colored surfaces will look.

After this first process of coloring, the motif is essentially crudely finished. Now it can be seen where more work has to be done; where surfaces need more points to look darker, where exact contours must be worked out, or where the motif looks too "flat." When this further work is done and colored, only details should remain to be worked out.

White on Black

White scrimshaw on a black background is, in principle, made in the same way, with the difference that one must think "the other way around." In black scrimshaw, one works out the dark parts of the motif, while in white scrimshaw one must cut or punch the light parts and "lights" of the motif. For transferring the motif, I would suggest going back to the pointing technique.

A whale on a buffalo horn, made by Eva Halat on a knife by Eberhard Kaljumae.

Colored Scrimshaw

I would recommend, in any case, that a beginner start with single-color work, since the basics can be learned best that way. The subject of "colored scrimshaw" should thus be explained only in principle, since very individual techniques come into use here.

In the 1980s, well-known scrimshaw studios in the USA developed the technique for colored scrimshaw to its highest point. Every artist developed his own style, which differed from others mainly in nuances. This is also true of the present-day scene. Some work in color with almost black contours, others use only very subdued color tones. There are also works that equal the finest miniature oil painting. They are made so gracefully that the naked eye cannot see any points or lines.

The basic techniques of colored scrimshaw are the same as those of black-white work,

though colored scrimshaw work is much more intensive. Here the motif is not formed from worked and unworked surfaces; here all the surfaces must be brought to life with needle and color—except those that are to remain white.

A good aid for "cracking" colored scrimshaw is a loupe with at least 4x magnification; a stereo microscope is even better. So that the finished scrimshaw does not look like a blurred photograph, the adjoining areas of different colors must be separated precisely from each other. Thus the contours should be pointed very neatly and closely. I point the colored surfaces individually and then color them in order.

The biggest difference from single-color scrimshaw —except the greater time required—consists of the coloring. While one can simply rub the color of monochrome work in, the coloring of multicolored ob-

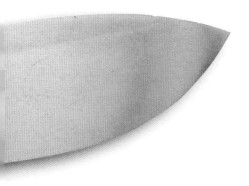

jects must be applied very, very carefully with a fine-pointed brush (at best, size 0 or 00). I like to use oil paint; it is not as thin as water color and thus can be controlled better. The removal of excess paint must also be done with the greatest caution, so that the adjacent, differently colored area does not accidentally take on an unwanted color. A cotton swab or the edge of a paper napkin twisted into a point are very good for practical work.

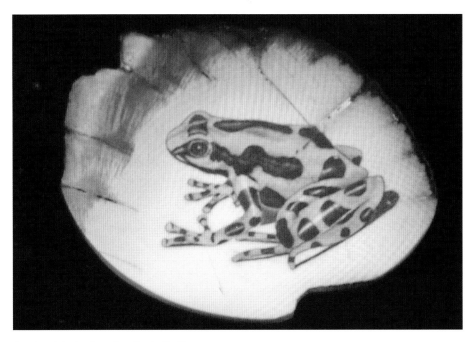

A colored Scrimshaw frog by Attila Harmat.

Coloring of Titanium

Stefan Steigerwald

Titanium alloys gained entry into knifemaking in the early 1980s. Two American knifemakers, Bob Terzuola and Michael Walker, did pioneering work here. In Germany it was Christian Wimpf who made this material eligible for the salon with all its colorful splendor. It was then built into the still-modern *Linerlock* folding knives (with locking springs). Light weight, good rigidity, and splendid optics speak for this material. Interestingly, the natural gray of titanium can be altered into bright colors. The physical property of so-called *optical interference* is utilized: When light is reflected several times, color effects are created. An oil film on water is a good example of it. The light is reflected at various levels and creates different colors. The distance between the reflection levels influences the colors. The surface of titanium is one of the surfaces, and the oxide layer, which is created intentionally by the treatment described below, is the other reflection surface.

Titanium and the oxygen in the air form a very thin, transparent oxide layer. This layer is so thin that it does not change the color. A color change only appears when the thickness of the oxide layer increases. The oxide layer can be strengthened by anodic oxidation or heating, and then—abracadabra—the striking colors appear.

Titanium screws, anodically colored. The colors result from different tensions. The numbers indicate the volts of tension.

If one passes electricity through an electrolyte (an electricity-conducting liquid), oxygen forms on the positive electrode (anode) and hydrogen on the negative (cathode). Oxygen reacts very freely and creates an oxide layer on the reaction surface—here on the titanium. This layer is firmly attached to the metal, but tends to wear off from use. Thus it is advisable to attach parts made of colored titanium so that they can be removed for further work (for example, screw them on).

A non-conducting container to hold the electrolyte is needed. A suitable electrolyte is a 10% solution of ammonium sulfate. As a cathode, we need a nearly equally large piece of titanium. This source of voltage determines the color. If one wants to create only blue colors, a 12-volt auto battery or a charger with a power of at least two amperes will suffice. Other colors require higher voltage. For this, one needs an adjustable power pack. *Be careful with higher voltages! Be absolutely sure of good isolation, and avoid open fires (no smoking!).* Hydrogen that is formed in the coloring process can ignite. The piece of titanium must be absolutely free of grease and completely immersed in the electrolytic liquid. Also, no other metal parts may be attached to the object.

When the power is turned on, one can observe how gas bubbles arise. The color appears very quickly.

Rigid knives, as well as folding ones can be decorated with screws, especially when they are made of colored titanium. Knife: S. Dammann, Damasteel® blade, ivory handle.

Work Safety

Before we start to work, here are a few important safety tips. In knifemaking there ironclad rule: "Safety comes first." This is in the nature of the thing, since one is, first working with sharp objects; second, is working with machines; and third, comes int tact with dust and other dangerous substances.

The following tips come from daily practice but do not claim to be complete. They c release the hobbyist from his duty of being careful.

- Essentially, before attaching the handle, **wrap the blade with tape.** Thus one kil flies with one stroke. The tape protects the worker from cuts and the blade from scra and other damage.
- Always wear suitable **safety goggles** when working on machines and when using so and acids.
- Work with **acids** only **outdoors.**
- When working with solvents, acids, and adhesives, **provide sufficient ventilation.**
- When doing work that makes dust, **always wear a dust mask.** Your respiratory s will thank you. Some woods, such as cocobolo, can induce strong allergic reaction

Making Knives Yourself

Why should one go to the trouble of making a knife himself when the dealers' show windows and catalogs are overflowing with knives of the most varied natures, shapes, and materials? There are many reasons. I'll mention a few that have moved me to practice this fascinating hobby. First of all, there is the almost sensual pleasure of creating something with one's own hands, being able to touch it, use it, and take pleasure in it, because it is beautiful and feels good. Many people no longer work at occupations where they produce tangible results, meaning that in the evening they cannot touch what they have produced during the day. Here some of the pleasure in work surely is lost. When I have made a new knife, I carry it with me for a time. I feel it and enjoy the feeling. Second is the work with elegant and interesting, often exotic, materials whose variety cannot be exceeded. I think of fossil bones or mammoth ivory, where one holds pieces of our earth's history, thousands of years old, in his hands. Fine woods, shimmering shells, artistic Damascus steel, mysterious iron from space, the most modern materials from the world of aerospace—the knifemaker can use all of them. The next point is the use of tools and the learning and using of production methods. Here one is part of a tradition that is as old as the history of mankind. Cutting tools were the first utensils that our ancestors made of stone. The knifemaker brings his own creativity into the making of a knife. He makes a knife according to a pattern, a unique piece, the only one in the world. And not least, which is not so often the case with other hobbies, he can earn money with his hobby—if he can separate himself from his knife at all and wants to sell it. And now let's get on with it.

Making a Full-tang Knife

Using a Kit

There are four basic ways to produce a knife blade:
- Forging, the most traditional way,
- Filing, the most time-consuming way,
- Grinding with a belt grinder,
- Milling.

This section goes into detail about the making of a knife by using a kit, such as are available in specialty shops. The expert may pass over these lines. The beginner is having a "schedule" placed in his hands, with the help of which he can make a knife.

Knifemaker Richard Spitzl files a blade.

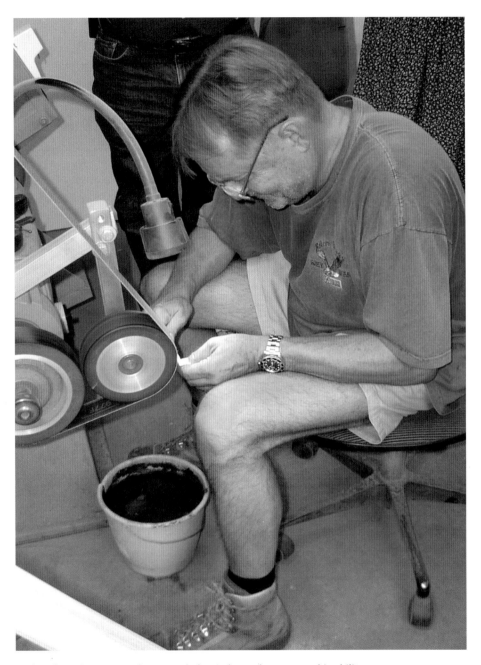

Knifemaker Dietmar Kressler uses a belt grinder to demonstrate his ability.

Tip: The publishers and authors cannot accept any responsibility for the incorrect use of the tools, machines, materials, or techniques described below.

The kit consists of the blade, the guard element, the rivet bars, and the lanyard tube.

The blade is prepared, meaning that the shape is set, the holes for the rivets are drilled, the steel is polished and the blade is sharpened.

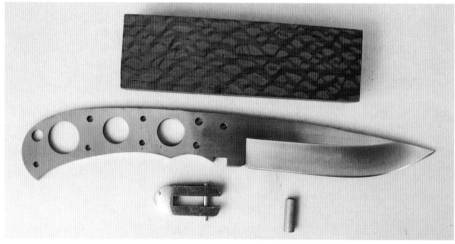

The kit.

The Basic Equipment

Here are the most necessary tools and aids:

Files
The least that one needs are one flat and one half-round file. Key files are helpful for fine work. Universal files are the most useful. For rough woodwork one can, of course, use wood files.

It is basically advisable not to use the files for steel and other metals on other materials. That means, for example, that one or more files should be reserved exclusively for use on steel. The results speak for themselves.

Vise
A so-called *mechanic's vise* (see photo) is ideally suited for knifemaking. The vise can

Key files..

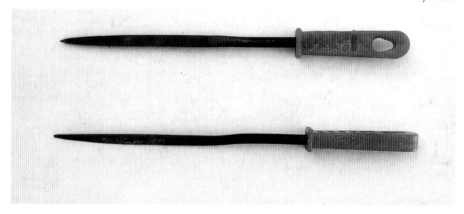

Grinding discs.

Grinding Cylinders

Grinding cylinders are coverings of emery cloth that are stuck onto a rubber roller and fixed with a screw mechanism. The roller is fixed in the chuck of an electric drill. If need be, one can do without them and do the work on the radius with a half-round file, but better-looking surfaces are made only with grinding cylinders.

be turned in all directions and thus eases the all-around working of the knife.

Emery Cloth

See page 62 and page 151 in the "Working the Surface of Steel and Wood" section.

In working with emery cloth, it is helpful to tear the cloth into narrow strips. Then it is placed over the blade of a file and held with one finger. Now pass the file with the cloth over the worked piece like a file.

Mechanic's vise.

Electric Drill
A rugged drill press is ideal. A hand drill in a rack, such as one can buy anywhere, is also useful. One must, of course, accept their higher level of noise.

Hack saw

Hammer

Adhesive
Two-component glues have proved themselves.

The tools, machines and aids described here for use in making a knife from a kit are not necessarily obligatory, but very helpful and time-saving.

Polishing Set
Whoever wants to add glitter to handles and fittings does best with a polishing set, such as are available in the trade. The sets consist of polishing materials in stick form, a sisal brush, and a felt or cloth disc.

The set is used as follows: The brush is fixed in the chuck of a drill. The drill is set for high speed, the polishing material is held against the brush so that the brush takes it up. The area to be polished is held against the brush.

For wood or horn, the use of a brush is usually sufficient. Metal can be polished to a high gloss with the felt and/or cloth disc.

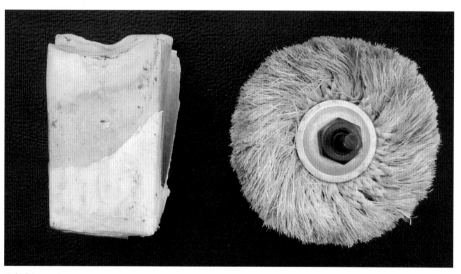

Polishing set.

Belt Grinder

Hardware stores sell quite reasonably priced belt grinders for use in the home workshop. The use of a belt grinder saves time, but does not have any decisive influence on the quality of a product.

Work Processes

The first step is also the most important: Wrap the blade in tape so that it is completely covered up to the handle section. Again: This should prevent the blade from being damaged during the work, and more importantly, the knifemaker should not be injured by it. Scarred fingers do not belong among the identifying marks of a successful knifemaker.

The next step is the fitting of the guard piece. In this case, the guard piece is attached in the vise from the bottom and then riveted. A tip as to balance: The handle of the knife should be lighter than the blade area. To attain this, one can taper the guard piece or the tangs and boreholes or apply the tang.

In the guard piece and the blade, there are holes for attaching the rivet rods. When boring the guard piece, ridges are formed on the inside and must be removed.

With a flat file, the ridge on the inside of the guard piece is removed.

Use a flat key file for this. Carefully remove the ridges and be sure not to hold the file at an angle. Otherwise the edges would be rounded and the guard piece will not fit neatly onto the blade. A visible gap between the blade and the guard piece would result.

One should definitely be sure to avoid gaps or make them as invisible as possible. A lack of gaps says a lot about the quality of the handiwork in the knife. Quite apart from the fact that visible gaps indicate careless work, dirt and moisture gather in gaps that can lead to corrosion in time.

When the ridges are removed, the guard piece is pushed onto the blade and the rivet rod is put in. Since the rivet rod is always longer than necessary, it is shortened to the right length. The rod should project 2 mm on each side. After the rod has been filed or cut to length, it is put in again and riveted. Do not forget to line up the guard piece from the side, so that it is not at an angle.

Hold the blade so that the end of the rod projecting from the guard piece is on a hard surface (iron plate, anvil or vise head) and rivet the other end with deliberate hammer strokes so that the projecting end is hammered flat.

Riveting the guard piece.

To seal the space between the guard piece and the blade, one can apply quick-drying glue where the two touch. Capillary action sucks the glue into the gap and thus seals it as protection against moisture. A drop of weapon oil can do the same on a finished knife.

Now it is time to prepare the handle material. It is important that the material is absolutely flat on the side that will lie against the knife. This problem is solved most elegantly by using ready-made handle panels (from the trade). When cutting your own wooden, horn, or bone pieces, take the time to file or smooth the surfaces evenly. Belt or cup grinders do a good job here.

The two handle pieces are now filed or sanded on the outsides, where they meet the guard piece at right angles. This rules out a gap between the handle panels and the guard piece.

Now the two handle panels are placed on the angle and the contour of the handle is transferred to the handle material with a pencil. To set off the grip panels with color, fiber material can be placed between the metal and wood.

The fiber is marked.

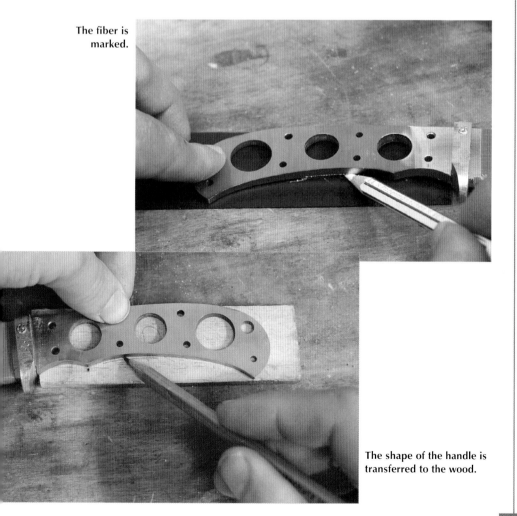

The shape of the handle is transferred to the wood.

Then we cut out the contour.

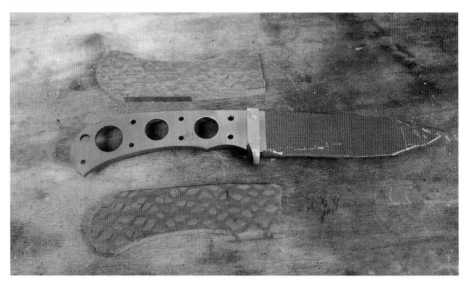

The two halves of the handle are cut out..

The next step is the gluing of the handle panels. First, though, bore a number of dead-end holes in the sides of the handle panels that face the metal. Use wood or metal drills with a diameter of 5 or 6 mm.

Boring dead-end holes to hold the adhesive.

The holes (don't drill too deep, just 1 to 2 mm!) serve to hold the glue and enlarge the gluing surface. In attaching the flat angle against the similarly flat handle material (one of the two handle panels), enough glue remains in the holes to assure a really firm grip.

Before gluing, roughen the angle with coarse filing lines and degrease it with alcohol or acetone. The surface must be completely free of grease and dust.

Mix and apply the two-component glue as the maker directs. Press lightly and fasten with clamps.

The wood is held with clamps after being coated with glue.

After the glue has hardened, remove the clamps and bore holes for the rivets and the tube for the lanyard. The holes already drilled in the tang serve as guides.

Drilling the holes for the rivets and lanyard tube in the glued half of the handle.

Now the second handle piece can be glued on. After hardening, the rivet holes are bored the rest of the way by using the already bored holes as guides. A note about the hole diameter: I drill the holes for the rivets and the lanyard tube 1/10 mm larger than the rivets and tube. The rivets and tube should slide into the handle material without particular pressure. Since the rivets and the tube will be glued later, it is not necessary to press the parts firmly into the material. The pressure created by pressing them can result in cracks, either in the riveting process or later, if the material shrinks, as wood, horn and other organic materials tend to change their volume under changed environmental conditions. Handle panels were formerly riveted right to the tang, which is no longer necessary with today's efficient adhesives.

The second half of the handle is drilled through the holes in the first half.

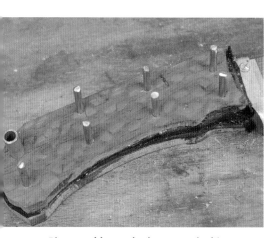

Rivets and lanyard tube are pushed in.

The rivet rods should be roughed with abrasive and degreased before being glued.

Again: It is not a good idea to rivet the handle panels to the tang with a hammer.

Fastening the Handle—Tips for the Experienced

Nothing is as constant as change. This also refers in a negative sense to knife production. Since natural materials like wood or horn are usually combined with metal here, the transition places are a problem. Natural materials behave differently than metals, and cracks or steps can result at the transitions. Experience in working with the materials and care in planning and working play an important role in reducing or eliminating such ugly faults.

In making the handle, one proceeds from the finished blade with all its boreholes for the fastening elements, and perhaps the lanyard loop. The surface of the tang must be clean and degreased. Usually the front side of the tang is closed by the guard piece or the bolster. In a fully integral knife, there are two attachments for the handle material. The attachments can be made differently: cutting back—angled off to the inside—is the so-called *dovetail fitting*. The advantage of the dovetail is that the handle material is practically wedged in and has no chance of coming out toward the top. A straight joint is simpler to make, especially when one is not using a milling machine. Joints with curves are hard to make but decrease the danger of breakage under high pressure, since the notch effect is reduced by the curves.

Ideally, handle panels made of natural material should be cut some time before being worked, then left alone, so that tensions in the material can decrease.

When gluing the handle panels to the tang, no strong pressure—such as with screwdrivers—should be used, since this can cause tension in the material that work out negatively over time. Two-component glues have proved themselves, and so have thin liquid quick-drying glues. It is true here that grease is the enemy of all glues, so carefully degrease the gluing surfaces.

High-performance glues hold out well, so the question is justified: Is further attachment necessary at all? In our opinion, yes.

For dovetail joints, thin rods are sufficient, since the joint holds the handle material.

If one still wants to play it safe, as with knives that will take heavy use, screwing the handle panels in addition to gluing them is advisable.

In the "Riveting" section from page 39 on, the common screw connections are portrayed. In addition to these screws, normal countersunk screws can be used. For a better appearance, one can sink them somewhat more deeply and then cover them with other, better-looking materials. So-called *mosaic pins* are recommended. Or, as described above, homemade inlays of any desired material can be glued in and then smoothed even with the handle material.

Rivets that are hammered in and pressed together (*cutlery rivets*) are used in kitchen knives and nostalgic western-style knives. They are not suitable for hardwoods, since the pressing and the resulting tension in the wood can lead to cracks over time. The heads of the rivets are not very high, so that it can happen that with further working of the handle too much is removed and the head comes loose.

Rivet rods are good-looking. They are usually glued in the edge areas of the handles and give additional support. A tube at the end of the handle to hold a lanyard to secure the knife, also gives added support.

Now the handle panels are worked with files and emery cloth so that they give the right "hand feeling." A knife should fit into the hand so well that even after long work, it does not become uncomfortable, but can still be held securely and firmly. In this step, even the beginner can give the knife his own individual style. Beginners often make the mistake of making their knife handles too voluminous. A handle as thick as a soda bottle not only looks awkward, but also becomes uncomfortable over time while working. Then too, it is too heavy.

Pearls for the Belt

One can make pearls for the belt from wood, horn, ivory or other materials with simple work processes. Cut the material crudely to the desired size, drill through them, and carefully turn a somewhat larger wood screw into the hole. Tighten the screw in the chuck of a drill. At medium speed, shape the material in the desired form with file and emery cloth, and polish it. Do not put on too much pressure, so that the part does not come loose from the screw.

Curves are best ground with a sanding drum..

The handle contour is filed ...

... and worked with the emory cloth.

When the handle has the desired form, one can finally polish the handle panels. Here the polishing set from the hardware store is put to use.

Another tip: Small cracks or splits in the handle can be touched up with polishable glue (such as acrylic or quick-setting glue). Fill the crack with a drop of glue, let it dry, and then smooth and polish the place. Larger faults can be covered with glue into which sanding dust from the original material had been mixed.

Whoever decides for natural wood can treat it with an oil finish. This procedure is time-consuming, but worthwhile.

Use cooked linseed oil mixed with turpentine. Source: art shops. Brush the wood with a paintbrush and let it dry a few days. Then smooth the wood with fine steel wool, coat it again and let it dry. Repeat this process (including smoothing) several times. Finally polish it manually, using an old woolen sock. This time-honored method not only provides a nicer appearance, but also creates a wonderfully warm and pleasant feeling. The oil can penetrate deeply if one puts the knife in a jar or glass filled with linseed oil.

The handle material is saturated in a jar full of linseed oil.

Round Handle Inlays

Whoever likes round handle inlays can proceed as follows: Make a dead-end hole (a hole that does not go completely through the material) with a drill of the desired diameter. Attach the material for the inlay (such as mother-of-pearl) to a piece of round steel, German silver or brass of the same diameter as the hole. Put the round metal piece in the chuck of a drill, run it fairly slowly, and use a file to remove enough material so the inlay matches the size of the round metal. Clean it up with emery cloth, separate it carefully from the metal with a blade, and the piece can be inlaid.

The finished knife.

Tips for Surface Treatment

Polishing
The simplest means of surface treatment is polishing with wax. The wax is transferred to the sisal or polishing disc and the handle is polished with it. This works well with wood, bone, ivory, horn, etc.

Stabilized wood or horn, layered wood, micarta or artificial gemstones can, thanks to their acrylic-resin content, be brought to a high gloss without polishing materials.

Some woods, as described in the section on woods and their properties beginning on page 43, need sealing. For these woods, the best solution naturally would be to spend a little more money and buy the stabilized type.

How the professional polishes wood is described in the section on wood polishing, beginning on page 62.

Precise Smoothing
Individual blemishes on the surface can be removed without having to smooth the whole surface again. This can be done as follows: Remove a strip of emery cloth about 1 cm wide from the sheet. Lay the strip on the piece. Press the cloth with one finger precisely on the place under which the blemish is located. Now pull the cloth under the finger, maintaining the pressure on the cloth. The emery cloth will remove material precisely from the blemish. Repeat several times, but be careful, as dips can be formed in larger surface

Building a Curved-tang Knife

After the methods have been developed and tested on a kit knife, we can now venture to make a knife that is formed completely our own work.

As an example, I have chosen a knife with a curved tang or *Spitzerl*. These knives have the charm and the advantages that suitable horn or antler pieces can be worked into handles without much changing.

For this book I have chosen a piece of antelope horn as the handle material. Since we are making our own blade, we can match the geometry of the blade (length, width, height, bend, etc.) to that of the handle optimally. If one buys a finished blade, handle material that suits the blade must be found. Here it is the other way around; a nice piece of horn can be combined with a homemade blade to form a harmonious knife.

Our knife shall have a blade of nearly rust-free, powder-metallurgically produced *Damasteel* (see the section on Damascus steel beginning on page 18). The *Damasteel* looks very good along with the chosen antelope-horn handle. Granted, this steel is not cheap. But when one decides to make a knife himself, one should not scrimp on the choice of steel. Whoever is not so sure of his ability can naturally practice on lower-cost steel.

Antelope horn. The attachment places for the handle caps are already prepared.

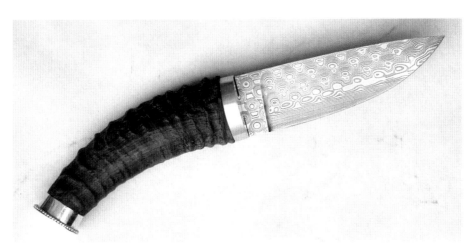

The finished knife.

The pattern and a piece of Damasteel.

For the blade shape, the choice fell on a hunting-knife blade. The first crude design for the blade was drawn on a piece of cardboard, out of which the pattern was cut with scissors.

Knifemaker Richard Spitz draws the blade outline.

With a needle or pencil, transfer the blade outline to the steel.

Now cut out the blade with a hack saw. Holes drilled in advance make the sawing easier. After sawing, the final contour of the blade is filed, or if one is at hand, ground on the belt grinder.

Filing the contour.

Belt grinders from the hardware store are relatively reasonably priced and well suited to hobby knifemaking. Now it is time to work out the angles on the knife blade. Here there are just two possibilities: grinding on the belt grinder or filing. Filing will appeal to the beginner, since grinding a blade on the belt grinder requires much practice and experience.

Before we begin filing, the center line on the future cutting edge must be marked.

This should prevent taking too much metal off one side in the "heat of battle," which would make a wavy and uneven cutting edge.

To mark the center line, measure the thickness of the steel and halve the result. Now blacken the cutting-edge area with a wide felt-tip pen and mark the halfway line with a compass.

Marking the center line.

Filing the tapers.

When the tapers are finished on both sides, the knife is worked with emery paper of ever-finer grain until the desired surface is attained. Now the blade can be sent to the hardener for hardening. For our blade I have specified 58-59 HRC (Rockwell) hardness. Important to the hardener are the material data, since the temperatures and times depend on it. In choosing a hardener, one should entrust his work to a business that has experience in hardening blades.

Since we want to accent the pattern of the Damascus steel, the blade is etched.

First it must be degreased with acetone or alcohol. The surface must be smoothed relatively finely. Grade 800 emery paper has proved to give good results.

A tall glass bottle serves to hold the etching fluid. It has proved useful to make a hole at the far end of the blade. Fasten a thin wire here, by which you can hang the blade in the etching medium.

Etching with Battery Acid or Iron Trichloride

Battery acid is a very good etching medium and can be bought at an auto-parts store. To speed up the etching process, the acid can be warmed by placing the glass, filled to about 4 cm of the rim, in a water bath and slowly warming it to 60 to 70 degrees Celsius. It is important that if this is done in a closed room, a window must be opened! On principle, I etch only in the open air. I also advise, for various reasons, that one not work with acid in living quarters. When working with acid, definitely wear gloves and protective goggles, and follow all the instructions for using dangerous materials.

The etching process takes several minutes, depending on the temperature. It is advisable to take the blade out of the acid after a few minutes and check the depth of the etching. Remove the loosened particles from the blade with a damp cloth at the same time. The rest of the etching goes faster. But don't inhale the fumes!

All the desired effects can be attained, from a light pattern on the surface to relief depths. When the desired depth is attained, rinse the blade with water and put it in a natron bath (some baking powder stirred in water) for a few minutes to neutralize the acid. Then smooth the surface carefully with 2000 grade emery paper and a suitable smoothing block. Finally, polish it with polishing paste and a soft cloth and oil it.

Etching with Iron Trichloride
Iron trichloride is also useful for etching. Art shops or electronic shops sell it in the form of powder or small pieces. Copper engravers use it to etch their printing plates.

Dissolve the iron trichloride in warm water until the solution is saturated, and then hang the blade in the liquid. Iron trichloride does not create fumes or eat into clothing or skin, but it makes unsightly spots on cloth—one cannot have everything.

The blade in an etching bath.

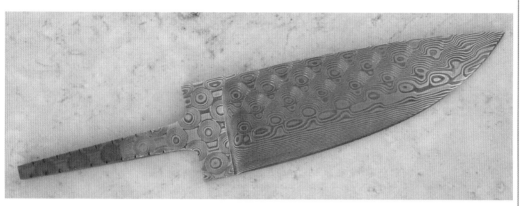

The etched blade.

Preparing the Tang

After the blade is finished, the handle and cover plate must be prepared. To fit the tang into the horn, it is necessary to make a slit in the horn. To prepare for this, measure the width and height of the blade at the transition from the blade to the tang. Transfer the dimensions to the front of the horn where the blade is to be inserted.

We bore holes with drills that have the same diameter as the tang is thick, one just below another in the marked field.
The length of the holes should equal the length of the tang plus 2 to 4 mm.

The remaining material between the holes can be removed with a specially developed tool, which can be had in the trade.

Keyhole saw.

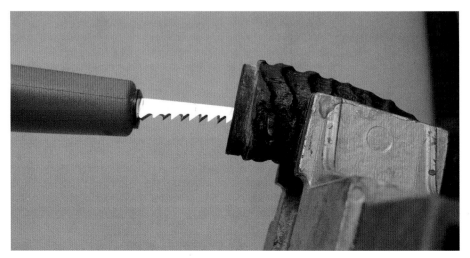

The keyhole saw in action.

It is also possible to make a small saw yourself by cutting a saw blade for a hack saw to shape with an angle cutter (Flex) or grinder.

What remains after the sawing can be removed with key files.
When the tang fits into the slit, one can glue the blade right in, or make a covering piece of sheet metal or some other material. For this, we use a thicker sheet metal (2 to 3 mm thick), place the handle with its front to the metal, and trace the outline of the handle. We saw the piece out oversize and mark the lines of the tang cross-section onto the center of the sheet.

As with the slit in the horn, we bore holes—but with a diameter that is somewhat smaller than the thickness of the tang, and we work out the slit carefully with a key file. We choose a smaller diameter because in-exactly drilled holes will otherwise make a crooked slit that will have to be broadened beyond the measurements of the tang. The blade would then have play and one could see through the gap between the blade and the sheet metal.

The work must be done very carefully, so that the blade is positioned exactly and, as noted above, no split results. Freedom from splits is the mark of good work. The specialist will start by checking the places where transitions exist for neat work.

When the blade fits, shake up the glue and apply it. To remove bits of glue from metal parts that are hard to reach or already completely polished, a simple homemade tool suffices. Flatten the end of a 2 to 3 mm thick brass rod and file it at an angle. Brass has the advantage of not causing any ugly scratches on the metal. Still, do it carefully.

A homemade tool to remove bits of glue.

Whoever wants an end cap can get it at a specialty shop or make it out of a piece of sheet metal, like the aforementioned cover plate, or of some other material.

Other contrasting materials like wooden or horn plates can also be made. One can also fit the blade into the handle by sawing through the wood block in the middle, grinding the plates straight, working the recess for the tang out of the two sides, and gluing the whole thing. It has only the disadvantage that the gluing surfaces must be exact. Despite all one's care, the gluing gap will remain visible.

Miniatures and Neck Knives

Miniatures

A special area in the realm of knifemaking is the making of miniatures. One cannot claim that they have any utilitarian value when they are less than 1/10 the size of an original knife. It might be, though, that one would want to dissect a mouse. But the makers of classic knives are often amazed at what graceful works of art take shape in the workshops of the miniature specialists with a great deal of patience and love for detail. Although—or precisely because—these knives are tiny, they require just as much work as their big sisters. Transitions and fittings must be carried out very carefully. Sometimes special holders or modified tools are needed. When choosing materials, one should consider the size of the knife. Essentially, only finely structured, dense material is suitable. Such miniature knives will probably remain very exclusive, often expensive decorative and unique works. For they are made only by demanding handcrafting.

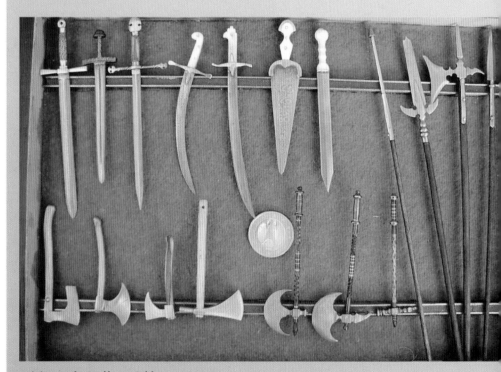

Miniatures by Wolfgang Schlag.

Neck Knives

Between the miniatures and the "normal" knives are the so-called *neck knives*, small knives that one can wear on a chain or cord around the neck. An art that is still useful.

The knives shown here were made by the author's two daughters, 11 and 14 years old. To make filing the blades easer, wedge-shaped rolled steel, available in the trade, was used to make the blades.

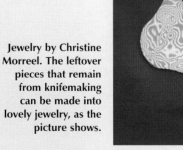

Knives made by Sabrina and Isabella Hellwig.

Jewelry by Christine Morreel. The leftover pieces that remain from knifemaking can be made into lovely jewelry, as the picture shows.

Polishing Steel

The polishing of metal surfaces is probably the most work-intensive process in knife-making. Here only capable work leads to good results.

Emery cloth and paper can be had in various qualities. The use of store-bought goods had proved itself. Recommended are *3M, VSM* and *Klingspor*. These brands have a high-quality grit binding, meaning that the grit is linked strongly with the carrier material and does not come loose quickly. Besides, the distribution is better; the gains are distributed evenly. Tests with low-value goods cost only time and give unsatisfactory results. Here one would save at the wrong place. For coarser abrasive work, emery cloth with 60, 80, 120, 180 and 240 grains has proved itself. If finer grain is needed, try wet-dry sandpaper with 600, 800, 1000, 1200 and 2000 grains. The number indicates how many grains are attached per square inch of the carrier. The higher the number, the finer the sandpaper.

Experience plays an important role in smoothing surfaces. Here on paper, only the basics can be given. In this case too, testing is better than studying.

Not every type can be smoothed equally well. An RWL34 gives fewer problems than an ATS34, although the RWL34 contains more carbide. The absolute tops in sandpaper wear are powder-metallurgic steels like CPM-S30-V and CPM-S90-V (ex-CPM440-V and CPM420-V). Later too, they are still durable.

In the workshop the sandpaper should be stored divided by grain. Good light is important (halogen has proved itself). Only in problem-free light can it be seen whether the traces of the previous work process have all been removed. Only then should one go on to the finer grain.

Variously shaped blocks can be used for sanding. They protect the fingers, and really flat surfaces can be formed only with them.

The best grain for beginning sanding depends on the quality of the surface that was created in the preliminary work. If it was filed, 80 or 120 grain is appropriate. If the blade comes fresh from a belt grinder with a 120-grain belt, one can proceed with 240 grain. Many knifemakers grind and polish everything by machine to the end. Here one sees clearly how far the spectrum of working possibilities extends.

But let us go back to the filed blade. Filing is usually done perpendicular to the blade. To be able to see clearly whether all the faults are removed, one must smooth along the blade. For this one uses a sanding block, so that the paper is pressed on really smoothly. If one has already smoothed everything with 120 paper, one can go on with the next grade, at best 240, at a right angle to the former direction. The steps between the grains should not be too great, or too small either. The following steps have proved themselves: 120, 240, 400, 600, 800, 1200 and 2000, or 180, 320, 600, 800, 1200 and 2000.

With satin finish one can stop with 600 grade. It is important that when changing grades, the smoothing direction must also be changed. Thus one sees whether the marks of the previous smoothing have been removed.

Do not forget the spine of the knife when smoothing. Here too, it should look good. Take a good look at the angles and transitions. They should be ground neatly and cleanly angled, which is not so simple. Here the signs of quality are seen in a finished knife.

Now the question arises: Satin finish or high-gloss polish? The right preparation is needed for both finishes. Satin finish is made by sliding the emery paper evenly over the surface in straight lines at the end. The emery paper should lie completely flat.

A sanding block with a hard rubber surface performs good service here. But be careful with transitions so they do not get rounded. It is a matter of taste which grade one stops with. The 600 grade gives a nice finish. One can also combine 400 with 1200; that means begin with 400 and then finish with 1200. Many knifemakers also use sanding paste or sanding pads.

For high-gloss polishing, the preliminary work is very important. Smooth the surface as fine as possible up to grade 2000. Only after that can you carefully use the soft to medium polishing disc on the polishing machine. A fine polishing paste is a good store-bought polishing material for a high-gloss polish.

When polishing, do not press on the angles. We don't want our blade to be rounded. But that can happen with excessive polishing. Neatness is important, so that single grains of grit do not get into the polishing disc and spoil the nice polish. A high-gloss blade takes a lot of work, but often the whole glory is gone after a single ordinary bread-slicing. The reader may have noticed that the author is not a great friend of these sensitive surfaces of carbon steel. High-gloss polish was an effective corrosion guard for carbon-steel knives, but this is no longer needed for chrome steel.

There still remains the question of to what grain the smoothing should go before hardening. This depends on the steel and the type of hardening.

For rust-free steel that is hardened in a vacuum oven, there is no tinder layer on the surface. Thus one can smooth it a long way. Everything that can be done to unhardened steel is done more easily by hand. If the blade is to have a satin finish, one can, in principle, finish smoothing the surface. After hardening, one need only rework it slightly. If a high-gloss polish is wanted, one stops after the 1200 grain and goes on after the hardening. Carbon steels are usually hardened differently from rust-free types,

for example, in a smithy fire, and build up a layer of tinder. So it does not make sense to finish the surface before hardening. Here one should stop after the 400 grain and continue after the hardening.

Whoever has decided on his type of steel will find the most suitable individual procedure over time. As said, there is no patented recipe, but here only the basic things should be noted.

Sharpening the Knife

One sharpens a new blade only after the hardening is finished. That means that in making the blade some 0.2 to 0.6 mm has been left in the area of the cutting edge. If one ground the blade fine before the hardening, the heat could cause unwanted changes. Then the steel's good qualities would be lost.

Many professionals sharpen the blade with a diamond file. Again and again one hears of people who make the edge on the belt grinder. *You are urgently urged not to do this with an ordinary store-bought belt grinder.* These machines simply run too fast. The resulting friction heat is enough to take the hardness out of the steel. Belt grinders with regulated speeds are much better for making the edge, but only when they run very slowly. But here too, only the experienced individual should try it. It is not easy to make the same angle on both sides of the blade. A blade can be ground fairly quickly.

A grinding set with adjustable grinding angles is recommended for the newcomer. Thus the angle can be kept easily on both sides and will not change, as can happen easily in freehand grinding. Then too, one can choose a flatter or steeper angle for the knife, depending on gusto and use. For coarser work, a steeper angle is recommended. If razor quality is wanted, then a flatter angle should be chosen.

Knife fans can spend a lot of money on high-priced Japanese whetstones, with which one grinds freehand. This work takes a lot of practice and care.

When the blade is sharpened, a ridge results, which can be very resistant, especially in highly alloyed steel. To get rid of it, there are various possibilities: One can work the cutting edge on the felt or polishing disc with polishing material, or turn to an old-fashioned leather belt fastened to a piece of wood.

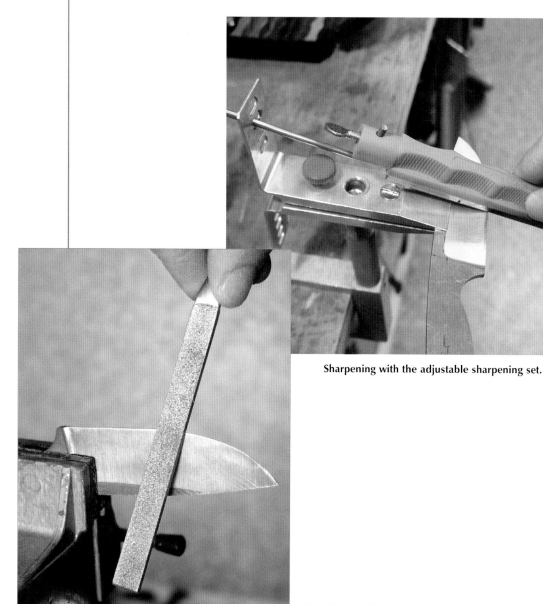

Sharpening with the adjustable sharpening set.

The diamond file in action.

How can you test whether the knife is sharp? There are several methods: Shave your upper arm, test it on a fingernail or the hair at the back of your neck, cut string, and so on. A test with a sheet of typewriter paper has proved to be very practical. Hold a corner of the paper with two fingers and then cut the sheet diagonally. If this can be done with a smooth cut, without tearing, the knife is sharp.

Whetting on a stone.

Stropping on a leather belt..

Side Trip:
Mechanisms of Jackknives

Stefan Steigerwald

There are countless inventions that involve jackknives. The various closing mechanisms are an interesting collecting area. An especially refined and clever closing system has a particular charm for knifemakers and knife fans.

The subject of jackknives can fill volumes. In the available space it is impossible to introduce all the mechanisms and variations. We shall limit ourselves to the basic mechanisms and their special features, and we also want to shed some light in the darkness of prevailing British concepts of subject and model.

Jackknives with complicated mechanisms should be able to be dismantled, so dirt can be removed most easily. It is important that the dismantling be simple to do and that

one has suitable tools for the job. Which tool will be needed and how one dismantles the knife should be learned when one buys it. An improper dismantling with an unsuitable tool can easily do great damage to the knife. For complex designs, the rule is: *"Never touch a running system,"* which means be glad that it works and leave it alone.

Individual parts of dismantling systems are usually interchangeable, and the blade movement is adjustable. This involves some handle material that neither suits nor pleases. Added engraving or surface treatment can likewise be added or undertaken more easily: Anodizing of titanium blades and other parts, gilding of opening pins or levers and distance rollers.

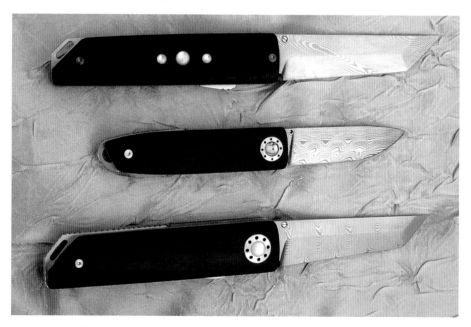

Three knives with locking-spring closings, by Franz Hutzler.

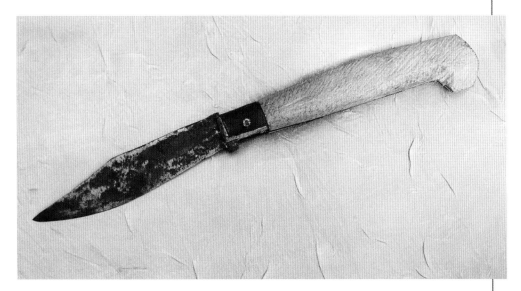

An old jackknife of the *friction folder* **principle.**

Above, a medieval discovery; below, a jackknife that has also survived for some years.

Friction Folder

The word *friction* involves rubbing; *folder* refers to a jackknife. One could simply designate this type as a knife without a rigid blade. The folding blade moves between its opened and closed positions just through friction between the handle and blade. In other words, the position supplies enough pressure to make the blade stay in place, but also lets it fold and unfold easily. The blade play must be sufficient. As a rule, though, it cannot be adjusted.

Friction folders, because of their simple mechanics, are easy to produce. This should not obscure the fact that there are noble and exclusive examples.

An especially elaborate knife by Ralf Hoffmann, with pink ivory panels and Damascus blade, open ...

... and closed.

In the further development, surely also conditioned by so many unpleasant injuries, clever technicians invented additional stops for the blade. The French Opinel and Laguiole knives provide good examples of this. Both knife brands were formerly classic friction folders. The Opinel had its characteristic turning ring, which held the blade steady in a simple manner.

The Laguiole, on the other hand, had a back spring that rested directly on the back of the blade at the level of the axis.

A modern jackknife that is also intended for use should have a lock. Here the *backlock* and the *linerlock* systems have prevailed.

A classic: The French Opinel.

Back Lock

This term indicates a jackknife with a *backward* or *back-spring lock*. Here the cooperation between the blade and locking lever must work very precisely. Only the most exact fitting results in play-free positioning of the blade. The locking lever takes its position audibly when opening, and the blade moves the last few millimeters of the way by itself when closing, through the spring power of the closing system.

In practice, knives of this type should be dismantlable so they can be cleaned inside. The individual parts must be fitted together precisely and not project disturbingly in either their opened or closed position. Here the quality of the workmanship can be recognized clearly.

A well-made backlock knife has its own charm. The knifemaker must have put a lot of work into the design and production. Because of the many well-functioning individual parts, the system appears technically refined and noble. The client should give some notice, when buying it, to vertical and lateral play as well as to easy use. The positioning of the locking lever says much about the quality of the knife. There are said to be fans who have bought a knife just because of the sound of the blade coming to rest, which indicates outstanding workmanship...

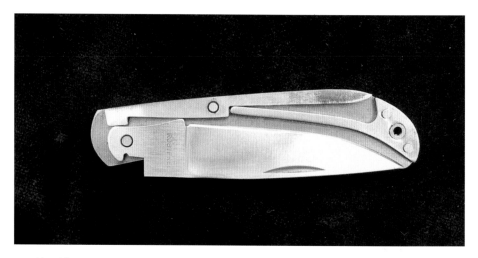

Knife with spring backlock, closed ...

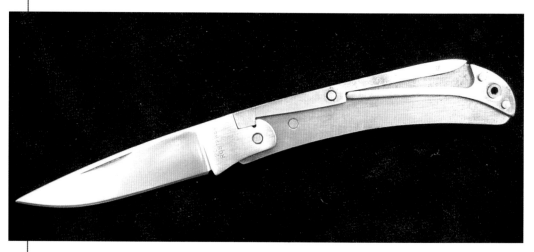

... and with opened blade.

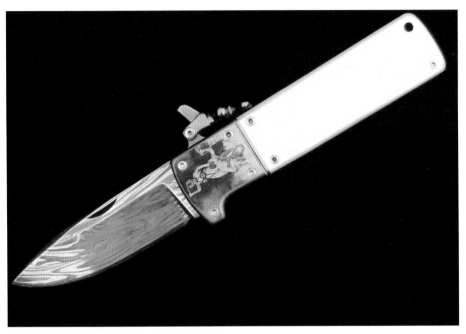

This knife with a backlock and lever was made by Stefan Steigerwald;
Ritchi Meier decorated it with an engraving.

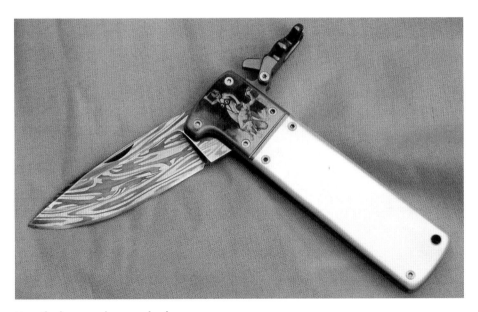

Here the lever can be seen clearly.

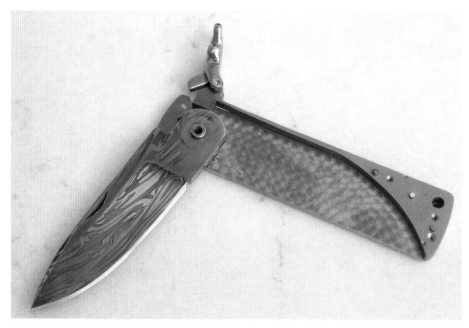

The same knife dismantled.

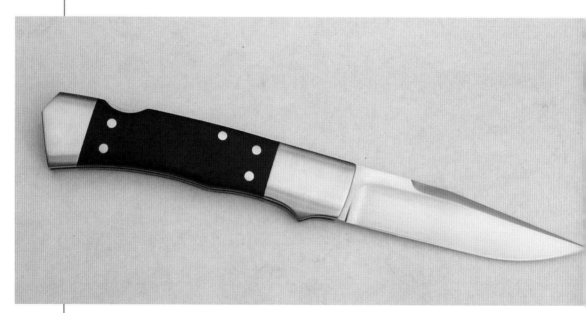

A knife with a backlock.

Linerlock

The *linerlock* concept indicates that the locking spring is integrated into the side panel—the *liner*. A ball or notch in the liner rests in a corresponding recess in the blade when closed; that means the spring with the ball holds the blade closed. This is the so-called *lock*. One can also describe the mechanics very simply with the term spring lock. It is easier to build than the backlock and thus also not so vulnerable. In spite of that, high-quality workmanship is required here too. The blade should move easily and play-free, the lock work gently, remain closed securely and be easy to open. The locking spring moves the blade the last bit of the way to its closed position and holds it there securely.

Since the *linerlocker* is often seen as a one-hand knife, the relationship of opening help to the handle and closing spring should be ergonomic.

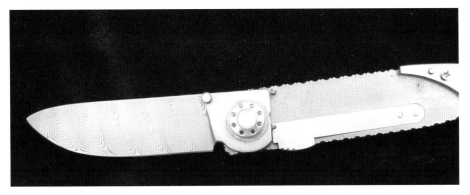

A dismantled jackknife with a locking spring (linerlock), offering a look at the mechanism.

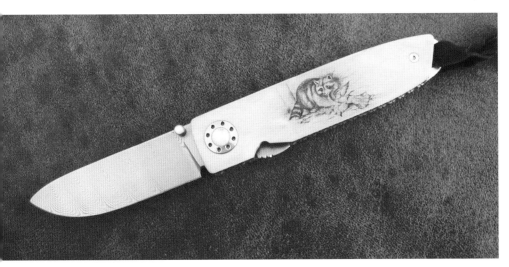

The same knife complete, made by Franz Hutzler.

A knife with a linerlock and panels of mammoth ivory, made by Franz
Hutzler and engraved by Kati Mau.

A knife by Kevin Wilkins, with titanium handle panels. The liner is anodized
and thus clearly contrasting in color.

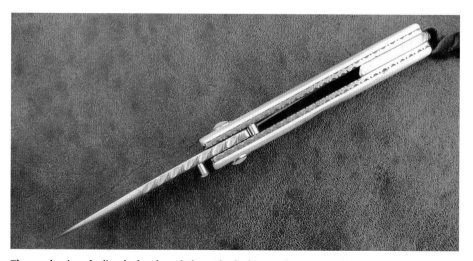

The mechanics of a linerlocker from below. The locking spring (a strip of sheet
metal) can be seen clearly.

In practice, the basic rule applies here too: The simpler the design and construction, the less vulnerable the mechanism. What does it help the hunter if can no longer close his jackknife after his "red work?" There are very sensible developments. The so-called *central lock* is one of them: With a high blade axis that includes balls, the blade is stopped. The axis is thus stopped from turning and linked with the handle. A small push button fitting into the axis con-trols the movement of the balls via a cone and a pressure spring. The balls fit into their recesses in the blade hole and lock it.

A similar variant is the so-called *Paul knife-lock*. The principle is the same, except that in place of the balls, a push button with a rest notch is used here. Both types require the highest precision in production.

The advantage is that the mechanism is extensively protected from dirt.

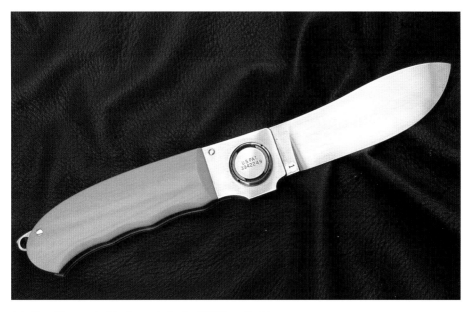

A knife with a central lock, made by Paul William Poehlmann.

A further development is the *radial lock* by Markus Becker. The well-mounted and spring-controlled locking lever is in the bla-de. The axis is firmly linked with the handle and has appropriate recesses into which the locking lever can extend.

The system is a variant of the linerlocker, and its production is very work-intensive. One can disagree as to whether such me-chanisms, that demand a lot of time and preparation, are necessary at all.

Whoever is excited by technology and holds such a knife in his hand is quickly convinced. Not everything has to be regar-ded from the standpoint of practical use; mechanics can also give pleasure.

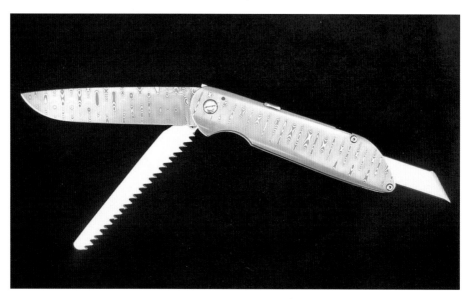

A knife with a radial lock, made by Markus Becker.

A good comparison from another realm involves watches. Mechanical watches are much more expensive and yet less precise than quartz watches. But the joy that comes from buying a beautiful handmade mechanical watch is much more pleasing to the connoisseur than a quartz watch.

The situation with handmade knives is similar. Individual pieces that required much handcrafting sometimes have slight deviations. But they give the knife a spirit.

5 Tips for Jackknife Builders

- *Prefer a screwed design, since the blade play can be adjusted and the knife can be dismantled for repairs.*
- *Pure titanium is a good plate material. It is light, can be colored anodically, and is relatively easy to work.*
- *Titanium alloys like Ti6-2-4-2 or Ti6V4 are suitable materials for the springs of spring locks.*
- *Steel 1.4034 with a hardness of ca. 45 HRC is recommended for backlock springs.*
- *Teflon plates between the blade and handle allow very soft blade movement.*

Reverse Lock

The reverse lock is basically built like the linerlock. The contact surface for the spring, though, is given a different position, so that the lock could be moved to the upper part of the knife, which should make unintentional unlocking less likely. Here too, one could debate on the sense or nonsense of this system. The basic structure, the order of assembly and the procedure need to be gotten used to. It is decisive whether one gets to know and enjoy this "somewhat different" design.

In any case, there are many versions of the classic linerlock type. A client's wish for ever-newer and better variants can result in designs that really were not necessary. The main thing is that it is something new.

Safelock

The *safelock* system is also based on the locking spring. The linerlock spring was lengthened toward the top and equipped with a control lever. The advantage is simpler operation. But there are also disadvantages. The tongue of the control lever, which is on top, is much longer than that of the normal linerlock. The easy servicing comes at the cost of the unlocking characteristic: The lever twists a little, until the whole thing goes into motion. Thus the process appears delayed and not customarily direct.

Safelock **lock construction. Detail: The long tongue to the unlocking lever is easy to see.**

Safelock, **lock construction. A preliminary model by Stefan Steigerwald.**

Linerlocker with Push Button

Here the locking spring is activated externally by a push button, which makes using it easier. The work of building it, to be sure, is not comparable to the results. The only advantage is that the knife looks like a knife with a push-button lock (see central lock), but still has a stable linerlock spring. From the back through the eye—but still good-looking.

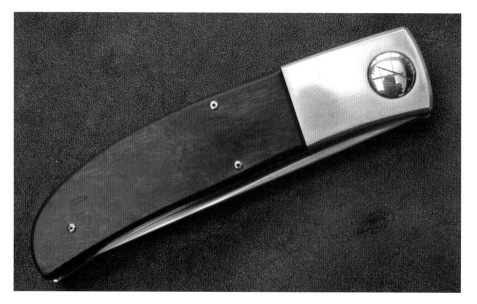

Linerlocker **with push button; knife by Mike Walker.**

Pushing Mechanisms

Small spring-operated levers mounted in the handle extend into recesses in the blade here. To the purchaser, the looks seem to stand out, since such systems are usually vulnerable. The precision of the fitting, especially of the lever, later governs the blade play. The mechanism is very vulnerable to wear and dirt. The collector is appealed to more here, since the very neatly made mechanism is visible.

Lever Lock

A spring-controlled lever rests in the blade. As with a pusher lock, exact movements for trouble-free functioning are necessary. This system actually offers no advantages over the normal back-spring lock (backlock). It looks better because of the small lever, which is no better or worse than any other "control lever" in use.

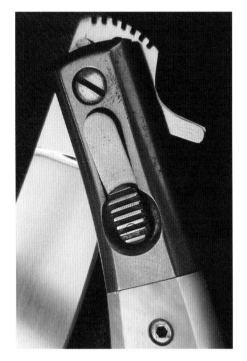

Lower left: A knife with a lever lock, by Bob Hayes.
Right: The Hayes knife half-opened ...
Lower right: ... and completely opened.

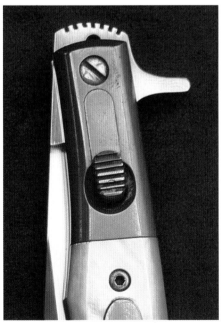

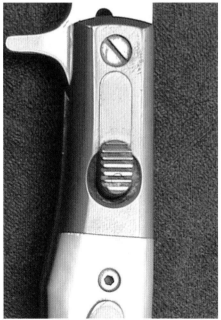

Motor Knife

The motor knife is a rarity. When one moves a switch, the knife opens or closes by means of a tiny electric motor. Surely a toy, but the technical work deserves respect.

In Conclusion

There are many types of locks. The names of many systems, derived from their inventors' or manufacturers' names, promised much and promoted sales, but are generally variations of standard types. What type pleases or serves for specific purposes is for the buyer to decide.

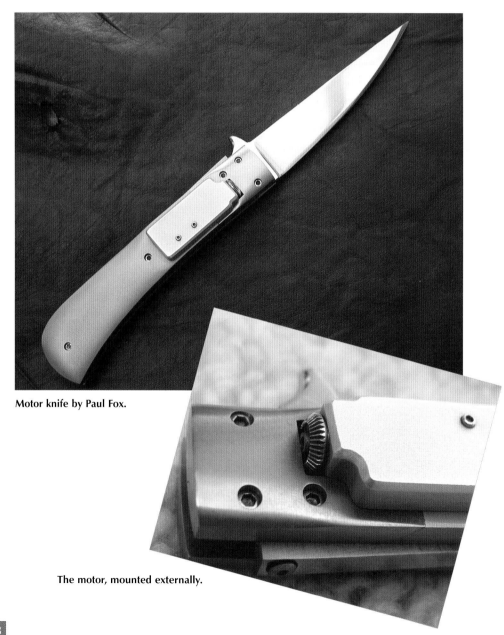

Motor knife by Paul Fox.

The motor, mounted externally.

Making Knife Sheaths

A sheath goes with a knife that has a fixed blade. It serves to protect both the knife and its owner from injury by the blade, as a housing place, and as a decoration.

The following directions describe the making of a quiver sheath of leather, one of the thermoplastic material Kydex, and touches on making a wooden sheath.

Leather Sheath (Quiver Sheath)

A piece of belt leather, 3 to 4 mm thick, taken from the back of cattle, is suitable for this. Naturally, vegetable-cured leather is preferred, since the vegetable dyestuffs are not as aggressive (to the blade) as the chemicals of chrome tanning.

Tools

The following tools are needed: an edge cutter, awl, ruler, compass, pocket knife, hollowing chisel, leather plane, cord, two needles with dull points, a hammer with a round striking surface, a punch, carpet cutter, folding bar, glue, leather coloring and a small brush. The work surface should be smooth and unpainted.

This picture shows the individual tools and aids; their use will now be described.

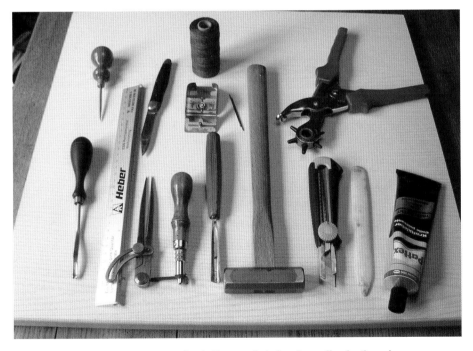

Edge cutter, awl, ruler, compass, pocket knife, punch, hole edge puller, leather plane, cord, two dull needles, rounded hammer, punch, carpet cutter, folding bar, glue, leather paint and small brush. The workplace should be smooth and unpainted.

A piece of cardboard serves as a pattern. First we draw a center line. The knife is placed about 1 cm from the center line. Then we draw the knife's shape with a gap of about 1 cm.

The outline is drawn and the sheath design is given a pleasing shape.

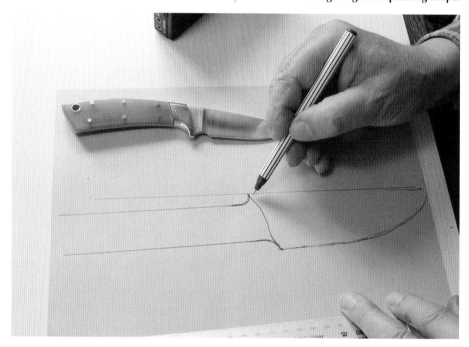

Now it must be decided whether the sheath is to have a belt attachment. For this project, an attachment was planned. Thus we continue the part of the sheath on which the belt will lie further upward. Then the pattern is cut out.

Fold the pattern along the center line, and then outline and cut out the other side

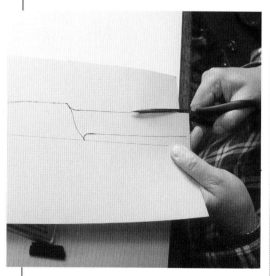

The pattern is cut out.

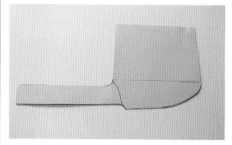

A cutout half.

The second half is drawn.

Using the finished pattern, the leather is cut. A carpet knife is ideal for this.

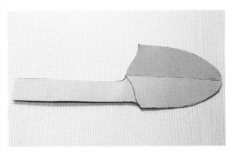

The finished pattern.

With the hole edge cutter, the cut is rounded. The resulting groove is important for the holes through which the cord will be pulled later. For optical reasons, we make a second groove 10 mm away.

The shape cut out of the leather.

With the hole edge cutter, the groove for the yarn is cut.

Now the holes are made with the smallest size of the punch. 2 mm is generally the smallest size on the market. The first hole is made.

The first hole is made.

Starting from the first hole, use the compass to mark all the other holes at intervals of 6 to 7 mm.

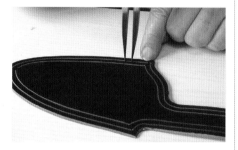

The compass marks the places for the holes.

The other holes are now punched at the marked places.

Punching the holes with the punch.

The holes are punched on one side.

Thin the leather at three places with a sharp knife: 1. At the end of the loop, so that the loop is not too thick; 2. at the bend in the loop, and 3. at the tip of the sheath. At the bend and the tip, several layers of leather will meet later, thus the leather should not be too thick there.

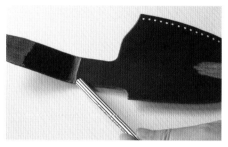

The leather is thinned with a sharp knife at three places.

Now the loop is glued with a good leather adhesive. Before the gluing is done, all light cut surfaces should be darkened with a dark leather coloring.

Darkening the leather at the light cuts.

When the glue has dried, the needed pressing power is applied with the hammer.

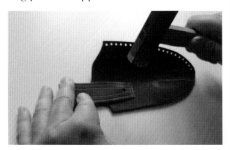

The loop is glued and the needed pressure applied with the hammer.

The so-called *spacer* is attached to the inside of the sheath. Important: Roughen the gluing places.

The spacer beside the sheath.

The spacer is roughened for gluing.

The leather of the sheath is roughened.

Knifemaker Erwin Schneller fits the sheath.

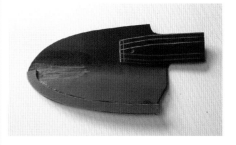

The spacer is glued in.

The spacer is punched along with one side of the sheath.

The spacer is punched on one side.

At the point, the spacer is made thinner with a sharp knife or the so-called *leather plane,* so that the sheath will not be too thick at this point. Tip: Leather planes can be found in knife shops. Balsa-wood planes used in modelmaking will also work.

The spacer is made thinner with a knife.

The leather plane is put to work.

The leather is now pierced from the back with the awl.

Use the awl to pierce the two sides along with the Keder.

Now the grooves on both sides are pulled together with the hole edge cutter, so they can take the yarn later.

Waxed perlon fiber is suitable as sewing yarn. It is not only very strong and resistant to environmental influences, but it also "brakes" itself through its strong waxing. The needles should be dull so as not to

The hole edge cutter is put to work.

damage the yarn while sewing. Begin sewing at the tip, with a so-called *saddler's stitch*.

Sew the saddler's stitch from both sides, using two needles.

The greatest pressure on the sheath is at the knife-insertion opening. Thus the knots are made there.

Making the knot.

The edges are now smoothed with the edge cutter.

Smoothing the edges with the edge cutter.

The side is cleaned up with a file, sandpaper or belt grinder, smoothed with the folding bar, and then coated with leather coloring. The sheath is finished.

The finished sheath with the knife it was made for.

A Sheath of Kydex

Sheaths made of Kydex* are becoming more and more popular for so-called *tactical action knives, combat, and survival knives.* The advantages of the plastic are obvious: Kydex is inexpensive, easy to take care of, insensitive, resistant and light. Kydex becomes soft under heating, so it can be shaped easily. The sheath can thus fit the knife's shape well. Since very thin material (1.5 mm) can be used, the sheath does not wear out. One need not worry about corrosion, as with a leather sheath (tannic acid residue!) when one keeps the knife in a Kydex sheath.

To make it, we need three pieces of Kydex, available in the knife trade. One piece each for the front and back, and one for the belt loop. The pressing is done on its own, by gluing a piece of isolating mat onto two boards. Two screw clamps provide the necessary pressure for the shaping.

At the beginning, the design is made.

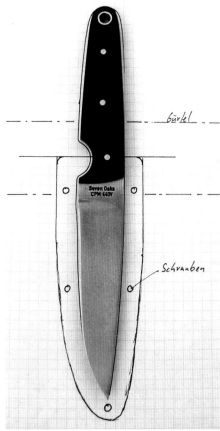

The knife with the design of the sheath.

The pressing apparatus.

---

* See also the section on Kydex in the standard work on action knives by Dietmar Pohl, *Tactical Action Knives: Development, Uses, models and Manufacturers.* 2nd edition, Motorbuch Verlag, Stuttgart, 2003, pp. 168ff.

From the design, the patterns for the two sides of the sheath are made.

The two pieces must now be heated to about 180 degrees C in a baking oven, until they are soft. With a preheated oven, this takes five to ten minutes.

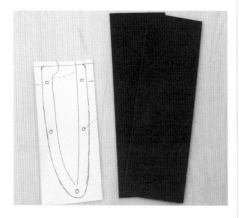

The Kydex plates with the design.

Now the work must go fast: Put the back piece on the board with the iso-mat, lay the knife on it, the front piece over it, the second board on top, put on the two clamps so the two Kydex pieces press on the knife and take shape.

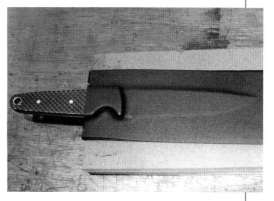

The two halves are fitted.

Now the belt loop is attached to the sheath in the same manner.

The belt loop is attached.

The knife with the two Kydex pieces clamped down.

The two halves can be glued or bolted, as in this case. Bolts can be removed, which can be an advantage, such as to clean the sheath when it has become dirty, which can happen in rough field action.

Finally, the final contour can be formed by cutting and smoothing on the belt grinder of filing.

But pure Kydex has one disadvantage: it scratches sensitive surfaces, even blades. This danger can be avoided by making the sheath with a lining of fine leather or cloth.

A Sheath Made of Wood

Japanese combat knives, called *Tantos* like the Samurai daggers, are usually, like their ancestors, kept in a wooden sheath. But for other knives too, the creative knifemaker can make sheaths of wood.

Making them is very simple. Select a suitable block of wood, saw it through the middle, smooth the sawn surfaces flat, and draw the shape of the knife on the two halves. Add a few millimeters to the outline and then cut it out with a chisel. Cut it deeply enough so that there is enough space for the blade. The front area must be worked very carefully, since the blade will be held fast there. This area can be lined with leather, so the blade will not be scratched when it slides into the sheath.

Finally the two halves are attached and glued.

The Kydex sheath with the knife, seen from the front ...

The kydex sheath with the knife, seen from the back.

Buying and Care of Knives

When you buy, the first impression is probably decisive. That is good. If one bought according to factual information and questions of quality, the whole thing would lack spirit. To be sure, every buyer should think about the quality of the workmanship and the choice of material, whether he seeks a utilitarian knife or a piece for the showcase.

The material that is used should be sturdy and easy to care for. As noted already, one or another natural product can cause problems. Unstable wood on a fully integral knife usually looks good only at the beginning. For full-tang and pocket knives too, low-shrinkage material should be used.

Another consideration when buying a knife is the maker. Does he have a good reputation for quality? Is he reliable about dealing with faults that appear subsequently? Does he have the same "wave length?" How good is his advice?

Organizations like the German Knifemakers' Guild have set high standards for quality and correct procedure with clients. The beginner can be helped by membership in the guild in choosing a knifemaker.

Here are a few points on the subject of quality:
Steel Choice: If it is not stated on the blade, ask for exact information. See the "Steels" chapter. Here it is said: Only the best steel is good enough.

Handle Material: Here too, look for good quality. Only the best material should be used for the work.
Blade Symmetry: Check carefully from all sides.

Fitting the Handle Material: Look for neat transitions and the smallest traces of glue. No cracks should be visible.

Surface Workmanship: Have all traces of the work been removed? Is the handle material worked neatly?
Collector's Value: Is the material of outstanding quality? Is it rare?
Sheath: The quality of the sheath is also important. How has the maker packed his product?

Maker: Does the knifemaker have a "name?"

A Few Tips for Fairs

Buying
The interested client avoids making the knifemaker nervous if he does not simply take the displayed pieces in his hand, but asks first whether he can pick them up for a closer look. With highly polished pieces or very filigreed works of art, this is not always granted willingly. Besides, a polite question is a good way to make a first contact.

Gripping or picking up knives by the blade is rude. What does the knife have a handle for? The knifemaker has to wipe or clean the blade afterward to make it presentable and immaculate.

Caution: The knives on sale are almost all sharpened for use, so that one could cut a finger with them. Checking their sharpness by shaving upper arm hairs is really unnecessary.

At fairs a lot is usually gong on, and the knifemaker is probably stressed. Often it is good, after a short discussion, to agree on a time to continue talking.

Obviously—at public fairs, business can be transacted. The interested party should not make the wares look bad. Knife fairs are not flea markets or rummage sales. On the other hand, the knifemaker should always be open to constructive criticism. Here, as always in life, the right tone matters.

Selling

If many visitors are thronging the display table, this is a sign of interest and a compliment to the knifemaker. He should always answer questions amiably.

A table overloaded with knives looks unprofessional. A nicely arranged and decorated selection is much more attractive.

Be careful with knife sheaths. A sheath is easily damaged or even ruined if the client is not careful. It is best if the knifemaker shows the sheath himself and does not take his eyes off the client when the client checks the goods.

Tips for Care

The worst thing anyone can do to a knife is to store it wrongly. Neither the bathroom nor the shelf over the heater is the right place to store knives.

Knives with handle panels of fresh wood are best kept in the humidor with the cigars ... But kidding aside, these are individual pieces of high value, and storing them wrongly can strongly decrease their values. As already noted, well-seasoned and properly sealed handle material, as far as natural products are concerned, is part of the basic requirements for maintaining the valúe of a knife. Yet one can never completely rule out the possibility of problems arising later in natural materials.

Overly dry storage is also bad for a knife. It is best to take the knife along on a walk or a hike now and then, as a second knife when hunting or fishing, so that it gets some fresh air, gets out of the usually too-dry inside atmosphere and "tanks up" a bit of moisture.

When the blade is used, the surface must suffer. It can be "freshened up" again, but how this is done depends on the steel and how it was worked. Only the experienced should restore knives using cleansing media, treat the knife with steel wool, emery cloth, or cotton wool. The knifemaker is the right man to ask and will surely help.

In caring for blades with oily materials, be careful to spare the handle, since these materials can make ivory, horn, or bone warp.

Wooden handles, though, can be freshened up with linseed oil or other wood-care products, and this includes the classical Damascus, but must be greased slightly with gun oil. After using the blade, clean it immediately and oil it anew. Cutting of very acidic fruit, like tomatoes or lemons, can leave ugly blotches on the blade. Roast pork also contains fatty acids that can lead to discoloration of the blade.

Knives should not be kept in their leather sheath for too long. The residue of tannic acid in the leather can attack the blade steel and handle fittings. The knife will become dull and the fittings will be blemished. Leather grease makes sheaths soft and flexible, and is thus just as unsuitable for their care as weapon oil.

Addresses

The following address list is made up of German specialists who, professionally or on the side, practice various handcrafting and artistic activities involving handmade knives.

The list does not claim to be complete, and all names are listed without a guarantee.

A	=	Association
M	=	Knifemaker
S	=	Smith
Sc	=	Scrimshaw dealer
G	=	Engraver
Sch	=	Jewelry dealer
E	=	Precious stone worker
Ma	=	Material dealer

Admiral Steel (Ma)
4152 W. 123rd Street, Alsip, IL 60803
800-323-7055
Email: terry@admiralsteel.com
Web: http://admiralsteel.com

Alpha Knife Supply (Ma)
425-868-5880
Email: chuck@alphaknifesupply.com
Web: http://www.alphaknifesupply.com/

American Bladesmith Society (A)
PO Box 1481, Cypress, TX 77410
Email: info@americanbladesmith.com
Web: http://www.americanbladesmith.com/

American Edged Products Manufacturers Association (A)
21165 Whitfield Place, #105, Potomac Falls, VA 20165
703-433-9281
Email: info@aepma.org
Web: http://www.aepma.org/

Arizona Custom Knives (M)
35 Miruela Avenue, St. Augustine, FL 32080
904-826-4178
Email: sharptalk@arizonacustomknives.com
Web: http://arizonacustomknives.com/

Australasian Knife Collectors (A)
PO Box 149, Chidlow 6556, Western Australia
618 9572 7255
Web: http://knivesaustralia.com.au/

Australian Knifemakers Guild (A)
Email: admin@akg.org.au
Web: http://www.akg.org.au/component/option,com_frontpage/Itemid,1/

Balbach, Markus (S, M)
Heinrich-Wörner-Straße 3,
35789 Laubus-Eschbach
(06475) 8911
www.schmiede-balbach.de

Becker, Markus (M)
Badener Straße 6, 76337 Waldbronn
(0171) 7 546 336
www-messer.innovationen.de

Big Antlers (Ma)
PO Box 1648, Pinedale, WY 82941
307-367-4398
Email: antlers@bigantlers.com
Web: http://www.bigantlers.com/

BladeSports International (M)
PO Box 205, Waxahachie, TX 75168
972 935-0899
Email: bladesports@bellsouth.net
Web: http://www.bladesports.org/

Brazilian Bladesmiths (S, M)
R. XI de Agosto, 107, CEP: 18270-000, Brazil
+55 15 32518092
Email: info@brazilianbladesmiths.com.br
Web: http://www.brazilianbladesmiths.com.br/

Brisa Knives, Inc. (M)
Hogbackavagen 20, 68600 JAKOBSTA, Finland
+358 6 7247815
Email: brisa@multi.fi
Web: https://www.brisa.fi/portal/index.php?option=com_frontpage&Itemid=1

Brownells (M)
200 South Front Street, Montezuma, IA 50171
641-623-5401
Web: http://brownells.com

Buck Collectors Club Inc. (A)
110 New Kent Drive, Goode,, VA 24556
Web: http://www.buckcollectorsclub.org/

Canadian Knifemaker's Guild (A)
RR #3, Bridgewater, Nova Scotia, Canada B4V
2W2
902-543-1373
Email: info@ckg.org
Web: http://www.ckg.org/

Case Classics Club (A)
28688 County Road 480, McMillan, MI 49853
Web: http://www.caseclassicsclub.com/

Chesapeake Bay Knife Club, Inc. (A)
939-I Berds Hill Road, Suite #122, Aberdeen,
MD 21001
410-272-2959
Web: http://www.knifeshows.com/clubs/cbkc/

Christmann, Jürgen (E)
Tiefensteiner Straße 19, 55758 Vollmersbach
(06781) 36 139
Juergen.Christmann@gmx.de

Classic Knife Kits (Ma)
881 Al Roberts Road, Senoia, GA 30276
877-255-6433
Email: info@knifekits.com
Web: http://www.knifekits.com/

Copper State Cutlery Association (A)
1294 E. Chelsea Dr., Queen Creek, AZ 85240
602-321-0421
Email: president@coppercutlery.com
Web: http://coppercutlery.com/

Crucible Steel Corporation (Ma)
1101 Avenue H East, Arlington, TX 76011
817-640-7777

Culpepper & Co., Inc.
PO Box 690, Otto, NC 28763
828-524-6842
Email: culpepperandco@verizon.net
Web: http://www.knifehandles.com/

Custom Kraft (M)
Box 3227, Riverview, FL 33568
813-671-0661
Web: http://www.rwcustomknives.com/

Custom Leather Knife Sheath Co. (Ma)
7024 W. Wells Street, Wauwatosa, WI 53213
414-771-6472
Email: rschrap@aol.com
Web: http://customsheaths.com

Cutlery Specialties (Ma)
6819 S. E. Sleepy Hollow Ln., Stuart, FL 34997
772-219-0436
Email: dennis13@aol.com
Web: http://www.restorationproduct.com/

Dammann, Steffen (M)
Waldstraße 4A, 91729 Gräfensteinberg
(09837) 976189

Dell, Wolfgang (M)
Am Alten Berg 9, 73277 Owen
(07021) 81 802
www.dell-knives.de

Deminie, Christian (S, M)
Hintere Gasse 41,
70825 Korntal-Münchingen 2
(07150) 41 668

Dietenhauser Ferdinand (M)
Schulstraße 8, 86565 Peutenhausen
(08252) 2876

Don Fogg Custom Knives (M)
Email: dfogg@dfoggknives.com
Web: http://www.dfoggknives.com/

Downie Knives (M)
10076 Estate Dr., Port Franks, Ontario, Canada
N0M2L0
519.243.2290

Eastern Pennsylania Knife Collectors Assn. (A)
Email: gep1@enter.net
Web: http://www.enter.net/~gep1/

Ebner, Johannes (S)
Pingitzerkai 2, A-5400 Hallein
(0043) 6245 80 454
www.johannesebner.com

Elen Hunting (M)
50 Battlehill Ave., Springfield, NJ 07081
973-379-5296
Email: elenhunting1@comcast.net
Web: http://www.elenhunting.com/

Elite Custom Knives (M)
1416 Locust St, Owensboro, KY 42301
270-926-4534
Email: rob@elitecustomknives.com
Web: http://elitecustomknives.com

Ellis Custom Knifeworks (M)
2900 Rennoc Rd., Knoxville, TN 37918
865-660-5280
Email: orders@EllisCustomKnifeworks.com
Web: http://www.elliscustomknifeworks.com/

Faust, Hans-Joachim (M)
Kirchgasse 10, 95497 Goldkronach
(09273) 6498
www.faustmesser.de

Fazalare International Enterprises (Ma)
Post Office Box 7062, Thousand Oaks, CA
91359
805-496-2002
Email: OurFaz@aol.com;%

Feodorow, Alexandra (G, Sc)
Schlegeleinswerth 26,
91541 Rothenburg o.d.T.
(09861) 87 881
www.af-gravuren.de

Fieck, Holger (M)
Hirschberger Straße 6, 38440 Wolfsburg
(05361) 34 806

Fifty Fifty Production (M)
P.O. Box 313, Turners, MO 65765

Fine Turnage Productions (M)
93 Fairfax Road, #1, Worcester, MA 01610
508-770-8072

Florida Knifemakers' Association (A)
1004 W. Socrum Loop Road, Lakeland, FL
33809
Web: http://www.floridaknifemakers.org/

Fort Meyers Knife Club (A)
P.O. Box 706, St. James City, FL 33956
Email: rsmegal@comcast.net
Web: http://www.geocities.com/mikegm.geo/
knifeclub.html

Geiger, Hans (M)
Heimatstraße 5, 77694 Kehl
(07853) 8287

Georgia Custom Knifemakers Guild (A)
Web: http://georgiaknifemakersguild.com/
home/modules/news/

Giraffe Bone, Inc. (Ma)
405-321-3614
Email: jerry@giraffebone.com
Web: http://www.giraffebone.co.za/web/de-
fault.asp

Glendo Corporation (Ma)
Post Office Box 1153, Emporia, KS 66801
620-343-1084
Email: glendo@glendo.com
Web: http://glendo.com

Göser, Jürgen (M)
Krumbacher Straße 2, 86491 Ebershausen
(08282) 61 512

Addresses

Gulf Breeze Firearms (Ma)
5253 Gulf Breeze Parkway, Gulf Breeze, FL
32563
850-932-4867
Email: gbf5253@bellsouth.net
Web: http:// www.gbfirearms.com

Haas, Andreas (M)
Am Rödchen 29, 65510 Jdstein
(0170) 8 175 957
www.haas-messer.de

Halat, Eva (Sc)
Obere Dorfstraße 30, 71576 Burgstetten
(07191) 85 033
www.evahalat.de

Hanneder Erich (M)
Eichbaumstraße 39, 85635 Höhenkirchen
(08102) 8171

Harmat, Attila (Sc)
H-7986 Kisdobsza, Fo u, 4. Ungarn
(0032) 73 348 396
www.attilascrimshaw@ttp.axelevo.hu
Harris Publications
1115 Broadway 8th Floor, New York, NY 10010

Hawkins Knifemaking Supplies (Ma)
110 Buckeye Road, Fayetteville, GA 30214
770-964-1023
Email: sales@hawkinsknifemakingsupplies.com
Web: http://hawkinsknifemakingsupplies.com

Heinle, Horst (Ma)
Frauenwaldstraße 5a, 61231 Bad Nauheim
(06032) 87 852
www.messer-spezial.de

Hoffmann, Ralf (M)
Forsterweg 108A, 22525 Hamburg
(040) 5402419

Hunting Society (A)
P.O. Box 173, Locust Valley, NY 11560
516 629-6052
Email: fgahagan1@yahoo.com
Web: http://www.huntingsociety.org/gunstocks.
html

Hutzler, Franz (M)
Pommernstraße 3a, 91413 Neustadt/Aisch
(09161) 5698

Iffland, Helmut (M)
v.-Eckert-Straße 13, 81827 München
(089) 4 300 183

International Blade Collectors Association (A)
700 East State Street, Iola, WI 54990
800-258-0929

Into The Wilderness Trading (Ma)
PO Box 1648, Pinedale, WY 82941
307-367-4398
Email: bags@wildernesstrading.com
Web: http://www.wildernesstrading.com/

Jankowski, Michael (M)
Sonnenburger Straße 64, 10437 Berlin
(030) 4 497 617
www.micknives.com

Jantz Supply (Ma)
309 West Main, Davis, OK 73030
800-351-8900
Email: jantz@jantzusa.com
Web: http://www.knifemaking.com

Jatagan
381 01 Cesky Krumlov, , Czech Republic
+420 775 22 6272
Email: mara@jatagan.eu
Web: http://www.jatagan.eu/

K&G Supply (Ma)
1972 Forest Ave, Lakeside, AZ 85929
Email: csinfo@knifeandgun.com
Web: http://www.knifeandgun.com

Kalumae, Eberhard (M)
Bremer Straße 38, 90765 Fürth
(0911) 7 395 537
www.custom-knives.de

Klein, Murat (M)
Zum Mückensee 7, 53567 Asbach

Klemm, Johann (M)
Im Weidig 20, 97702 Münnerstadt-Re-
ichenbach
(0973) 3251
www.messerklemm.de

Knife Collectors Club (A)
2900 S. 26th St., Rogers, AR 72758
479-631-0130
Web: http://www.k-c-c.com/

Knife Group Association of Oklahoma (A)
PO Box 1445, Tahlequah, OK 74465
918-456-1519
Email: kniffers@theknifegroup.com
Web: http://theknifegroup.com/

Knife World
Post Office Box 3395, Knoxville, TN 37927

KnifeLegends
124 Longwood Avenue Apartment #3,
Brookline, MA 02446
617-731-3499
Email: pshindler@comcast.net
Web: http://KnifeLegends.com

Knifemakers' Guild (A)
P.O. Box 1251, New Port Richey, FL 34656
Web: http://www.knifemakersguild.com/

Knifemakers Guild of Southern Africa (A)
Web: http://www.kgsa.co.za/

Knifemaker's Supplies & Tools (Ma)
5034 Jane Avenue, Brownsville, TX 78521
956-546-4861
Email: donwrobinson@earthlink.net
Web: http://home.earthlink.
net/~donwrobinson/knifemakerssupplies/index.
html

KnifeMakersDatabase.com, Corp. (A)
Long Island City, NY 11103
718-777-2120
Email: info@knifemakersdatabase.com
Web: http://www.knifemakersdatabase.com/
CustomKnivesKnifemakersDB.html

Kressler. Dietmar Fritz (M)
Brunnenweg 1, 28832 Achim
(0160) 5 941 810

Loquai, Gernot (M)
Odenwaldstraße 36,
65428 Rüsselsheim-Königstädten
(06142) 32 981
www.Loquai-Messer.de

Mader, Alfred (M)
Finkenweg 2, 89428 Syrgenstein
(09077) 8764

Maier, Richard (Ritchi) (G)
Schlesienstraße 29, 71069 Sindelfingen
(07031) 386 439
www.trompeter-ritchi.de

Masecraft Supply Company (Ma)
Post Office Box 423, Meriden, CT 06450
203-238-3049
Email: masecraft@masecraftsupply.necoxmail.
com;%

Mau, Kati (G)
Kälberzeil 34a, 98587 Steinbach-Hallenberg
(03684) 730 920
www.engraving-ma y.com

Midwest Knifemakers (M)
42112 Kerns Drive, North Mankato, MN 56003
507-947-3760
Email: service@midwestknifemakers.com
Web: http://www.usaknifemaker.com/

Montana Knifehandle Supply (MA)
68 Tahoe Drive, Kalispell, MT 59901
406-257-9310
Email: charles@saurknives.com;%

Addresses

Montana Knifemakers Association (A)
14440 Harpers Bridge Rd., Missoula, MT
59808
406-543-0845
Email: gmwknives@aol.com
Web: http://www.montanaknifemakers.com/

Morreel, Christine (Sch)
Badener Straße 6; 76332 Waldbrunn
(07243) 652 482
www.damastschmuck.de

Mother of Pearl Co., Inc. (Ma)
Post Office Box 445, Franklin, NC 28744
828-524-6842
Email: mopco@earthlink.net
Web: http://knifehandles.com

Narushima, Noriaki (M)
Unterhausmehring 9, 84405 Dorfen
(08081) 3299
www.nori-messer.de

National Knife Collectors Association (A)
P.O. Box 21070, Chattanooga, TN 37424
423-875-6009
Email: NKCALisa@hotmail.com
Web: http://www.nkcaknife.org/

National Rifle Association (A)
11250 Waples Mill Road, Fairfax, VA 22030
Web: http://www.nra.org/

Naturgalleriet ApS
Kongevejen 29, DK - 2840 Holte, Denmark
+45 45 42 01 23
Email: info@naturgalleriet.dk
Web: http://www.thegoodstuffshop.dk/

NC Tool Company (Ma)
6133 Hunt Road, Pleasant Garden, NC 27313
336-674-5654

Nordic Knives (Ma)
1634-C Copenhagen Drive, Solvang, CA 93463
805-688-3612
Email: info@nordicknives.com
Web: http://nordicknives.com

North Carolina Custom Knife Guild (A)
1015 Beck Road, Denton, NC 27239
336) 859-5486
Email: BlackTurtleFrg@aol.com
Web: http://www.ncknifeguild.org/

North Coast Knives (M)
17407 Puritas, Cleveland, OH 44135
Email: PJP@NorthCoastKnives.com
Web: http://www.northcoastknives.com/

Northeast Cutlery Collectors Association (A)
18 Hilltop Avenue, Gloversville, NY 12078
Email: agreen03nycap.rr.com
Web: http://www.ncca.info/

Northwest Knife Collectors (A)
10602 N.E. 60th Street, Kirkland, WA 98033
425-827-1644
Web: http://nwkc.org/

Ohnesorge, Gerd (M, Sc)
Pyrastraße 2, 06118 Halle/Saale
(0345) 5 201 034

Olbricht, Dhan (Ma)
Schmiedebergstraße 13, 34593 Knüllwald
(05686) 930 108
www.bladesandmore.de

Oregon Knife Collectors Association (OKCA)
Email: okca@oregonknifeclub.org
Web: http://www.oregonknifeclub.com/

Oso Famoso (M)
Post Office Box 654, Ben Lomond, CA 95005
Email: oso@osofamoso.com
Web: http://www.osofamoso.com/

Palmetto Cutlery Club (A)
P.O. Box 1356, Greer, SC 29652
Web: http://www.palmettocutleryclub.org/

Papke, Klaus (M)
Breite Straße 17, 41515 Grevenbroich 7
(02181) 9322

Peters Heat Treating, Inc (M)
Post Office Box 646, Meadville, PA 16335
814-333-1782
Email: lstall@petersheattreat.com
Web: http://petersheattreat.com

Pöhler, Joe (M)
Brettener Straße 101, 75438 Knittlingen
(07043) 31 607 oder (07082) 791661

Point Seven, Inc. (M)
810 Seneca Street, Toledo, OH 43608
419-243-8880
Email: pointseven@pointsevenstudios.com
Web: http://pointsevenstudios.com

Pop's Knives and Supplies (M, (Ma))
103 Oak Street, Washington, GA 30673
706-678-5408
Web: http://www.popsknifesupplies.com/index.
html

Queen Cutlery Collectors, Inc. (A)
P.O. Box 109, Titusville, PA 16354
Email: sales@queencutlerycollectors.com
Web: http://www.queencutlerycollectors.com/

Quintessential Cutlery (M)
136 Hazelton Street, Ridgefield Park, NJ 07660
201-641-8801
Email: gshaw@quintcut.com
Web: http://quintcut.com

Randall Knife Society (Ma)
P.O. Box 158, Meadows of Dan, VA 24120
276-952-2500
Email: payrks@gate.net
Web: http://www.randallknifesociety.com/

Rankl, Christian (M)
Possenhofener Straße 33, 81476 München
(089) 75 967 265

Rick Fields Ivory (Sc)
790 Tamerlane Street, Deltona, FL 32725
386-532-9070
Email: donaldgfields@earthlink.net;%

Rinkes, Siegfried (M)
Am Sortplatz 2, 91458 Markt-Erlbach
(09106) 251

Ritzer, Manfred (M)
Rosenstraße 10, 85757 Karlsfeld
(08131) 92 579

Riverside Machine (Ma)
201 W. Stillwell, DeQueen, AR 71832
870-642-7643
Email: uncleal@riversidemachine.net
Web: http://www.riversidemachine.net/

Rosinski, Jürgen (S)
Pater-Josef-Straße 8, 93303 Kelheim
(09441) 3107
www.messerschmiede-thaldorf.de

Ross Tyser Custom Knives (M)
Email: Ross@rtcustomknives.com
Web: http://www.rtcustomknives.com/

Rühl, Jürgen (S, M)
Pulverhäuser Weg 25; 64295 Darmstatt
(06151) 311 731
mruehl@t-online.de

Santa Fe Stoneworks, Inc. (M)
3790 Cerrillos Road, Santa Fe, NM 87507
505-471-3953
Email: knives@rt66.com
Web: http://santafestoneworks.com

Sarasota Knife Collectors Club (A)
Email: knifecollector@simplysarasota.com
Web: http://www.simplysarasota.com/KnifeCol-
lector/

Saviolo Publisher USA
Post Office Box 2675, Mandeville, LA 70470
985-792-0115
Email: SSJ@saviolopublisher.com
Web: http://saviolopublisher.com

SBC Enterprises
9 Mathew Court, Norwalk, CT 06851
203-838-8939

Schirmer, Werner (M)
Reuth 5, 96272 Hochstadt
(09574) 9078

Schlag, Wolfgang (M)
Karwendelstraße 11, 82140 Olching
(08142) 12 095
www.miniaturmesser.de

Schmalz, Fred (S, M)
Maingasse 2, 97478 Knetzgau
(09527) 591
www.damastschmiede.com

Schmidbauer, Heinrich (M)
Stelzhamer Straße 4, 94575 Windorf
(08544) 974 444
www.schmidbauer-messer.de

Schneider, Fritz (S, M)
Waldenserstraße 15, 76307 Karlsbad
(07202) 8052

Schneller, Erwin (M)
Feldstraße 29a, 82140 Olching
(08142) 12 407

Schramm, Horst (M)
Rathausstraße 32, 85757 Karlsfeld
(08131) 95 254

Schweikert, Andreas (S, M)
Riedsweg 26, 72116 Mössingen/Talheim
(07473) 6116
www.as-schmiede.de

Sheffield Knife Makers Supply, Inc.
Post Office Box 741107, Orange City, FL 32774
386-774-5754
Email: email@sheffieldsupply.com
Web: http://sheffieldsupply.com

Siebeneicher-Hellwig, Ernst G. (M)
Kleiststraße 13b, 85221 Dachau
(08131) 10 001
sevenoaks5@hotmail.com

Sinbad Glue Corp
806 15th Avenue West, Palmetto, FL 34221
877-332-1296

Solydwood Company
Post Office Box 06136, Bridgewater, NJ 08807

South Carolina Association of Knifemakers
Web: http://www.knifemakercentral.com/

Southern California Blades Knife Collectors Club
PO Box 1140, Lomita, CA 90717
Email: snsandsons@earthlink.net
Web: http://www.scblades.com/

Spitzl, Richard (M, Sch)
Wasserburger Straße 18, 85614 Kirchseon
(0174) 9 059 992
www.messer-spitzl.de

Spyderco, Inc.
Post Office Box 800, Golden, CO 80402
303-279-8383

Stamascus Knife Works Corp.
413 Fairhaven Drive , Taylors, SC 29687
276-994-8445
Email: danny.mcmanus@bigfoot.com
Web: http://www.stamascus-knife-works.com

Steigerwald, Stefan (M, Ma)
Schwander Straße 12a, 90530 Wendelstein
(09129) 402 151
www.steigerwald-messer.de

Steinwender, Karl (M)
Nelkenweg 11, 89584 Ehingen
(07391) 757 530

Stellar Rigs
Post Office Box 22132, West Palm Beach, FL
33416
561-616-5015
Email: info@stellarrigs.com
Web: http://www.stellarrigs.com

Stephen Bader & Company
Post Office Box 297, Valley Falls, NY 12185
518-753-4456
Email: badergrinder@hotmail.com
Web: http://stephenbadder.com

Texas Knifemakers and Collectors Association
P.O. Box 234, Eden, TX 76837
325-869-8821
Email: tkca@tkca.org
Web: http://www.tkca.org/

Texas Knifemaker's Supply
10649 Haddington # 180, Houston, TX 77043
713-461-8632
Email: sales@texasknife.com
Web: http://www.texasknife.com/

The American Bladesmith Society, Inc.
P O Box 1481, Cypress, TX 77410
Web: http://www.americanbladesmith.com/

The American Knife and Tool Institute
22 Vista View Ln, Cody, WY 82414
307-587-8296
Email: akti@akti.org
Web: http://www.akti.org/

The Curious House (P.), Ltd.
Director 42, Pratap Marg. Swaroop Sagar,
Rajastman , 313004, Udaipur
91-294-2529165
Email: pradeep@curioushouse.com;%

True North Knives
Post Office Box 176 Westmount Station, Mon-
treal, Quebec H3Z 2T2, Canada
514-748-9985
Email: neil@truenorthknives.com
Web: http://truenorthknives.com

Tru-Grit
760 E. Francis St. N, Ontario, CA 91761
909-923-4116
Email: Trugrit1@aol.com
Web: http://www.trugrit.com/

Universal Agencies Inc.
4690 South Old Peachtree Rd. Suite C, Norcross, GA 30071
678-969-9147
Email: info@uai.org
Web: http://www.knifesupplies.com/

Universal Agencies, Inc.
4690 South Old Peachtree Road, Norcross, GA
30071
678-969-9147
Email: cs@knifesupplies.com
Web: http://knifesupplies.com

Western Canada Knife Association
19861 114 B Ave., Pitt Meadows, BC, Canada
V3Y 1N3
604-465-5138
Email: ronnelson@shaw.ca
Web: http://www.wcka.org/

Wichmann, Ruth (G)
Swojeer Straße 7, 82140 Olching
(08142) 15 343

Wilbert, Guido (S)
R.-Schiestel-Straße 111, 66450 Bexbach/O.
(06826) 81 671

Wilkins, Kevin (M)
Kurfürstendamm 105, 10711 Berlin
(030) 8 922 506
www.wilkins-knives.com

Williamson County Knife Club
Email: williamsoncounty@yahoo.com
Web: http://w_c_k_c.tripod.com/williamson.
htm

Wolverine Knife Collectors Club
P.O. Box 52, Belleville, MI 48112
Web: http://www.wolverineknifecollectorsclub.
com/

Zirbes, Richard (M, Sc)
Neustraße 15, 54526 Landscheid-Niederkail
(06575) 1371

Photo Credits

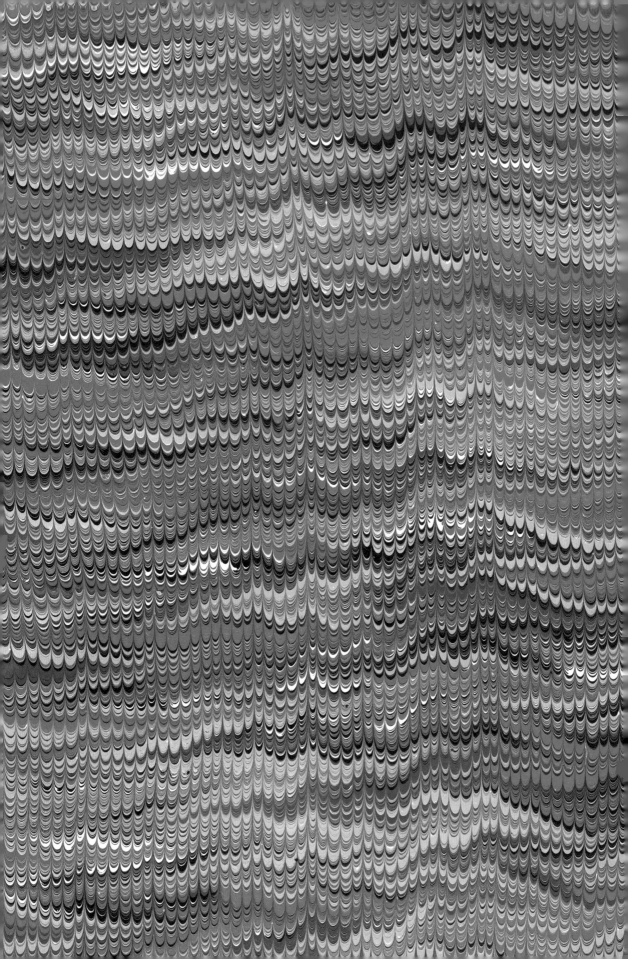